# FAITH
## and the
## MARVELOUS PROGRESS
## of
# SCIENCE

# FAITH

## and the
## MARVELOUS PROGRESS
## of
# SCIENCE

Edited by Brendan Leahy

**NCP**

NEW CITY PRESS
of the Focolare
Hyde Park, NY

Published in the United States by New City Press
202 Comforter Blvd., Hyde Park, NY 12538
www.newcitypress.com
©2014 Brendan Leahy

Cover design by Leandro de Leon.

Bible citations unless otherwise noted are from the New Revised
    Standard Version Bible, copyright 1989, Division of Christian
    Education of the National Council of the Churches of Christ in the
    United States of America.


Book layout by Steven Cordiviola


Library of Congress Cataloging-in-Publication Data

Faith and the marvelous progress of science / edited by Brendan Leahy.
    pages cm
  Includes bibliographical references.
  Summary: "This book contains ten reflections upon issues of
    importance in the world of faith and science. The contributors to
    this book write from a faith perspective but respectful of the place
    and role of science. Some write from direct scientific expertise
    while others draw on philosophical and theological perspectives"--
    Provided by publisher.
  ISBN 978-1-56548-514-3 (alk. paper)
  1. Religion and science. I. Leahy, Breandan, 1960-
  BL241.F34 2014
  201'.65--dc23
                              2014039615


Printed in the United States of America

# Contents

List of Contributors ........................................................... 7

Introduction ..................................................................... 9
   *Brendan Leahy*

## *Learning from History*

1. Common Historical Roots; Common Practitioners. 13
   *Brother Guy Consolmagno SJ*

2. Notes on the History of the Dialectic between
Scientific and Humanistic Knowing ......................... 31
   *Sergio Rondinara*

3. Chenu's Recovery of Theology as a Science ........... 53
   *Patricia Kelly*

## *Topics in Contemporary Debate*

4. A 'Cosmic Authority Problem'
Lawrence Krauss's and Thomas Nagel's
Approach to the Question of God ......................... 65
   *Brendan Purcell*

5. Modern Physics, the Beginning, and Creation ....... 91
   *Stephen M. Barr*

6. Science Is Not Scientific ..................................... 107
   *David Walsh*

7. Can it be Reasonable for a Scientist
to Believe in God? ............................................. 121
   *William Reville*

## Christian Perspectives on the Destiny of the Cosmos

8. Striving Towards the "Omega Point"
   Henri de Lubac on Pierre Teilhard de Chardin ...... 141
   *Noel O'Sullivan*

9. Do We Know Where We Are?
   Creation and the Trinity ................................................ 159
   *Brendan Leahy*

10. From Beginning to End: The Scientific Relevance of
    Creation and New Creation ....................................... 171
    *David Wilkinson*

# List of Contributors

*Stephen Barr* is a professor of Particle Physics in the Department of Physics and Astronomy at the University of Delaware, and a member of its Bartol Research Institute.

*Brother Guy J. Consolmagno*, SJ, is an American research astronomer and planetary scientist at the Vatican Observatory.

*Patricia Kelly* is Senior Lecturer in Catholic Studies at Leeds Trinity University, England.

*Brendan Leahy*, Bishop of Limerick, Ireland, and formerly Professor of Systematic Theology, St. Patrick's College, Maynooth.

*Noel O'Sullivan* is a lecturer in Systematic Theology at St. Patrick's College, Maynooth, Ireland.

*Brendan Purcell* is Adjunct Professor in Philosophy at Notre Dame University, Sydney, and assistant priest at St. Mary's Cathedral.

*William J. Reville* is Professor of Biochemistry at University College, Cork, Ireland.

*Sergio Rondinara*, Professor of Epistemology and Cosmology at the Sophia University Institute, Loppiano, Florence, Italy.

*David Walsh* is Professor of Politics at the Catholic University of American in Washington, DC.

*David Wilkinson* is Principal of St John's College and Professor in the Department of Theology and Religion, Durham University, England.

# Introduction

## Brendan Leahy

WRITING IN 1945, THE English mathematician and philosopher, Alfred North Whitehead commented that "...when we consider what religion is for mankind, and what science is, it is no exaggeration to say that the future course of history depends upon the decision of this generation as to the relations between them."[1] Describing the contours of these relations, Ian Barbour, the American scholar and Templeton prize-winner, proposes the following categories:[2] *conflict* (the Galileo case is often taken as an example), *integration* (this ranges from some theories of Intelligent Design to Process Theology), *independence* (here we can think of Karl Barth's theology and the scientist, Stephen Jay Gould's "non-overlapping magisteria"), and *dialogue*.

Many Christians today favor the approach of dialogue between faith and science. As Pope Francis writes, "all of society can be enriched thanks to this dialogue, which opens up new horizons for thought and expands the possibilities of reason."[3] After all, faith is not fearful of reason. It seeks and trusts reason. It values science for the simple reason that since there is only one Truth and since the light of reason and the light of faith both come from God, they cannot contradict each other. The

---

1. Alfred North Whitehead, *Science and the Modern World* (New York: MacMillan, 1925), p. 181.
2. I.G. Barbour, "Ways of Relating Science and Theology" in R.J. Russell, W.R. Stoeger and G.V. Coyne (eds.), *Physics, Philosophy and Theology: A Common Quest for Understanding* (Vatican, 1988), pp. 21–48.
3. Apostolic Letter, *Evangelii Gaudium (The Joy of the Gospel)* [24 November, 2013], n. 242.

Catholic Church's position, therefore, is that she has no wish to hold back the marvelous progress of science:

> On the contrary, she rejoices and even delights in acknowledging the enormous potential that God has given to the human mind. Whenever the sciences—rigorously focused on their specific field of inquiry—arrive at a conclusion which reason cannot refute, faith does not contradict it. Neither can believers claim that a scientific opinion which is attractive but not sufficiently verified has the same weight as a dogma of faith. At times some scientists have exceeded the limits of their scientific competence by making certain statements or claims. But here the problem is not with reason itself, but with the promotion of a particular ideology which blocks the path to authentic, serene and productive dialogue.[4]

Intrinsic to this dialogue is recognition that there are forms of knowledge other than those of the positive sciences. To reduce knowledge simply to what is known by empirical methods is called scientism or positivism. We can see scientism at work when we read Stephen Hawking and Leonard Mlodinow as they begin their *The Grand Design* by asking: "What is the nature of reality? Where did all this come from? Did the universe need a creator?" And then they go on to affirm, "Traditionally these are questions for philosophy, but philosophy is dead. Philosophy has not kept up with modern developments in science, particularly physics. Scientists have become the bearers of the torch for discovery in our quest for knowledge."[5] It is clear that for them there would be no room for an interaction of science and theology.

And yet the pathway of dialogue is needed, not least because it is linked to the promotion of peace and harmony in the world. It is possible to strive for "a synthesis between the responsible use of methods proper to the empirical sciences and other areas of knowledge such as philosophy, theology, as well as faith itself, which elevates us to the mystery transcending nature and human intelligence."[6] We need to recognize the many-sided

---

4. Ibid. n. 243.
5. Stephen Hawking and Leonard Mlodinow, *The Grand Design* (London: Bantam Press, 2010), 5.
6. *Evangelii Gaudium*, n. 243.

dimensions and ultimate mystery of the human person and our world striving for peaceful interdependence at all levels.

The contributors to this book write from a faith perspective but respectful of the place and role of science, both historically and today. Some write from direct scientific expertise while others draw on philosophical and theological perspectives to engage in reflection upon issues such as: how the division between faith and science arose; the nature of science; scientists and the phenomenon of atheism; the assumptions behind some contemporary debates; and the often-forgotten eschatological issues, the where-are-we-heading questions. It is hoped that readers will benefit from the many rich perspectives offered in these pages.

# 1

# Common Historical Roots; Common Practitioners

## Brother Guy Consolmagno SJ

AM A RELIGIOUS BROTHER in the Jesuit order; I have taken vows of poverty, chastity, and obedience to live in a community of priests and brothers doing the work the Church asks us to do. But I am also a scientist, an astronomer, a planetary geologist who specializes in the study of meteorites. I've got advanced degrees from MIT and Arizona; a few years ago I was elected the chair of the American Astronomical Society's Division for Planetary Scientists, the largest organization of planetary scientists in the world, and I have also served in a number of positions with the International Astronomical Union. I was even part of that group who demoted Pluto from planet status! I mention these things about myself, not to brag—or at least, not only to brag—but also to show that by my very existence I am proof that it is possible to be, at the same time, both a fanatic and a nerd.

I am a fanatic about my science. I love it; it is what I do. (And I am something of a nerd about my Church.)

A lot of people are puzzled by this fact. They think that science and religion are incompatible; after all, the idea of an eternal war between science and religion has been a popular theme in books and journalism for a long time. But two simple observations get lost in the noise. Science and religion have common historical roots: clearly this war has not in fact been eternal. And science and religion share common practitioners: at least for us, the two sides are not even at war. I'm one of those practitioners.

13

And so, just as a textbook uses "worked examples" to illustrate how different laws of physics manifest themselves in the real world, it is useful to take a look at some worked examples of how science and religion actually interact, and have interacted, in the lives of scientists, now and in the past; and in particular, in the history of astronomers like myself.

*Examples of how Science and Religion Interact*

To begin with, think about how astronomy manifests itself in the lives of ordinary people. The fact is, it hardly does at all. Though we all learned in school that the world is round, our own personal universe is flat, bounded by a few buildings or trees, with ourselves at the center of it all. We live our lives without ever experiencing that we're walking on the surface of a sphere...much less, that this world which seems so big to us is but an insignificant speck orbiting an average star in an average galaxy, one of billions of such stars and billions of such galaxies.

And, indeed, you might ask: do we need to know that? The writer of the opening chapter in Genesis described the universe as just such a disk covered by a dome; he knew nothing of modern astrophysics. But he knew God, and he lived a good and holy life. Isn't that enough for us?

I would argue, it is not. To be self-satisfied with our ignorance is to limit both ourselves and our relationship to God.

Consider the Book of *Job*. When Job, in his crisis, complains to God about the injustices he has endured, God responds in a fascinating way. Starting in Chapter 38, God asks Job if he knows all the wonders of the universe—wonders that Job had never thought about before. "Do you know the way to the dwelling of light? Do you know the laws of the sky?"

God asks this not to "show off" His greatness, nor even just to put Job's problems in perspective. Rather, there is implied an invitation: come with Him, to discover the way to the dwelling of light! Join with the morning stars who, we are told by the prophet Baruch, sang in chorus while all the sons of God shouted for joy at the foundation of the universe!

For those of us who are called to be scientists, the exploration of God's creation is a response to an invitation to spend time with the Creator. We get to play with Him, so to speak, uncovering the delightful puzzles He sets for us and marveling at the way the laws of the universe fit together with a logic that is both harmonious and elegant. In this way we learn to see a side of God's personality. Even if we are not professional scientists, we can still be fascinated by the workings of the universe that the professionals can share with us, and take part in the game at least as spectators.

In any event, it is clear that the one attitude we can never take toward science is fear, as if it were a threat to God. Speaking about science, Pope John Paul II put it most bluntly: "Truth does not contradict truth." Science does not replace God; rather, it reveals that God is more amazing than we could ever have realized. The writer of Genesis insisted that God made everything; everything that could be seen: the flat Earth, the dome above it, even the "waters above and below the dome." If today we recognize that the universe includes all the stars and galaxies, extending for 13.8 billion light years (and that's only the part we can see), how much bigger we must recognize God to be!

Speaking of domes...when I think about the history of the Church and its interaction with science, I am reminded again and again of the Church of St. Ignatius, a major center for the Jesuits in Rome, an edifice that has a strong connection with my own Jesuit-run institution of the Vatican Observatory. The building itself was designed in the 1600s by Father Orazio Grassi, a Jesuit priest who was also a mathematician and quite a good astronomer. In 1618, when three comets visible to the naked eye blazed across the skies, Grassi arranged with other Jesuit colleagues in Europe to observe them and their positions simultaneously, using telescopes. Recall, Galileo had only just introduced the telescope to the world of astronomy in 1609; no one had ever seen a comet through a telescope before. Certainly Galileo had not.

The results of Grassi's observations were published in a small booklet in 1619. He showed that the comet appeared in exactly the same position relative to the stars, whether observed in Rome or the north of Europe. Its lack of "parallax" proved that comets were quite far away; they really did orbit in space, beyond the orbit of the Moon. Since their motions were very odd compared to the planets, coming closer to the Sun and

Earth and then moving much farther away, this posed great challenges to everybody's theories (Ptolemy or Brahe or Copernicus) for how the planets moved.

Galileo himself refused to believe the evidence. He couldn't see how comet orbits like the ones Grassi inferred could be possible in the Sun-centered Copernicus system—he didn't know or understand Kepler's idea of elliptical orbits—and so he concluded that comets must merely be optical illusions in the Earth's atmosphere, like rainbows or Sun dogs.

Instead of accepting Grassi's evidence, Galileo made fun of Grassi and the way he had written up his results. Grassi wrote in the florid style of the times, tying his observations to the ideas of the ancient Greeks and Babylonians. Galileo wrote a book against Grassi, called *The Assayer*, where he insisted that one must rely only on the evidence of observation and experiment, not on the authority of the ancients or any other authority figure. Today this book by Galileo is considered the foundation of the scientific method, and rightly so. Ironically, Galileo asserted his point of view only on the basis of his own authority; he refused to accept the observations of comets that Grassi and his companions had made!

That was a shame. Among other things, it turned the Jesuits against Galileo. Before then, they had been among his strongest supporters. Father Clavius, the Jesuit priest who took part in Pope Gregory's reform of the Calendar in 1582 and taught mathematics at the Roman College (right next to St. Ignatius Church), had written letters of recommendation for Galileo when he was first looking for a job, and late in his life he even looked through Galileo's telescope at Jupiter and its moons.

And when Galileo was first called in to be questioned about his theories, it was under the care of the Jesuit Cardinal Robert Bellarmine, the greatest theologian of his time. After Bellarmine interviewed Galileo, he gave him a document certifying that Galileo was no heretic.

Bellarmine wasn't convinced of Galileo's science, however. The heliocentric system was a radical change, it would be like overthrowing Einstein today, and Bellarmine felt Galileo hadn't proved his point. (And in fact, Galileo hadn't. It would take another fifty years before Newton's theories showed how

Kepler's version of the Copernican system actually worked, and centuries before the motions of the Earth were finally directly observed.)

But Bellarmine did say something very interesting about Galileo and his ideas. Around the time of his interview with Galileo, Bellarmine wrote:

> If there were a true demonstration that the Sun was in the center of the universe and the earth in the third sphere, and that the Sun did not travel around the earth but the earth circled the Sun, then it would be necessary to proceed with great caution in explaining the passages of Scripture which seemed contrary, and we would rather have to say that we did not understand them than to say that something was false which has been demonstrated. But I do not believe that there is any such demonstration; none has been shown to me.

Here we see Bellarmine's openness to new ideas, and his realization that his understanding of Scripture might not be the last word. And we also see the sort of scientific skepticism that we honor among scientists. Clever ideas aren't enough: show me the evidence! The fact that, in the long run, Galileo was proved right and Bellarmine wrong was no fault of either, given the state of the evidence at the time. (And, incidentally, Cardinal Bellarmine is buried beneath an altar along the western wall of St. Ignatius Church.)

But the most notable astronomer associated with the Church of St. Ignatius is someone who specifically took advantage of a special characteristic of the dome on this church. The characteristic is that, in fact, there is no dome. When you walk inside and look up to where the dome ought to be, it looks real; but as you walk around the church and keep looking, you gradually realize that what you're seeing is a fake. They ran out of money; instead of building a dome, they put in a flat roof and then a few years later a Jesuit brother, Andrea Pozzo, painted the flat ceiling in a marvelous "trompe d'oeil" forced perspective, so that it looks just like a real dome...from certain points of view, anyway.

Since the church was built with massive pillars designed to hold the weight of a dome, but no dome itself, Father Angelo Secchi in the 1850's had the idea to put four telescopes on the roof of this church, one on each pillar. One of the telescopes marked the time each day when the Sun crossed the meridian; this was used to signal a cannon that would be fired so that everyone in town knew it was noontime. But the biggest telescope was used for some of the most important astronomical observations of the nineteenth century.

With this telescope, Father Secchi observed the planets, especially Jupiter and Mars, and he was the first person to describe them not as mere dots of light in the sky but as actual places, with clouds and weather and surface features. He used the term "canali" to describe some of the features on Mars; later other astronomers misinterpreted this word to imply that there were actual canals on Mars, and Martians who had built them. Secchi also did pioneering work on observing the Sun. Today there's a NASA spacecraft observing the Sun that gives Secchi the ultimate honor of using his name as an acronym for the Sun Earth Connection Coronal and Heliospheric Investigation package.

But the most remarkable work that Secchi did from the roof of that church was to put a prism in the light path of his large telescope and turn every dot of starlight into a rainbow of colors. He saw how different stars had different spectra, and he classified more than five thousand stars this way. And he knew how to interpret those spectra in terms of the elements present in those stars; for example, he discovered that some rare stars were rich in the element carbon.

Suddenly, astronomy was no longer measuring the mere position of the stars and planets. It became the study of what those stars and planets were made of, and how they got to be the way they are today. Father Secchi, from the roof of his church, became the father of astrophysics.

### Science as a Conversation with Other Scientists

Now, you may well ask, why was a priest like Father Secchi doing astronomy? For that matter, why was the Church concerned in any way with what a scientist like Galileo was writing?

In Galileo's day, science was still well embedded in the field of what was called Natural Philosophy. And the Church, who after all had invented and ran the medieval Universities, was in the position of what we sometimes call "the Academy," the received wisdom against which new ideas are tested. It had a responsibility to teach the truth as it knew it, and to protect against crazy ideas. That was especially important in those days when crazy ideas would lead to wars. (We tend to forget that the Galileo trial took place at the height of the Thirty Years War.)

It's no different today. (Except for the wars.) To get a scientific paper published you need to pass it by a series of anonymous referees, experts in the field who will judge if the paper is free from major errors and worth publishing. I have been a referee many times; and I have been refereed myself, many times. On more than one occasion the referees have stopped me from publishing a paper I'd submitted; and thank heavens. They have found many errors that I had missed. I am thankful to these referees. They've saved me from making a fool of myself in print.

We need referees because we aren't always right. We make mistakes. And referees remind us that science, like philosophy, like religion, is not something we do alone. We do it as a part of a community.

Science is not a big book of facts; it is a conversation with other scientists. To have a conversation, you need a common language, so that when I say "porphyritic type two olivine chondrules in a carbonaceous chondrite fall" the other meteorite scientists know exactly what sort of material I am talking about. That's one of the important reasons we study at universities—not to learn the facts, which anyone could do just from reading books, but to learn the language by living and working in the world of science where that language is spoken and alive, where we can grasp all the subtle shadings of meaning that no book can teach us.

And having a conversation means that to do science you have to do the sort of work that other people are interested in. You can't have a conversation if no one is listening. That also means you have to take the time to be around and to listen to the others, as well.

You know, we get a lot of letters at the Observatory from people who are working alone in their attics and who think they have discovered some new secret of the universe that the rest of us may have missed. It's very sad. They want to make the big breakthrough that will make them famous; or at least they want to be part of the wonderful fun of playing in God's Creation. But of course, most everything they write to us is nonsense. And even if, buried in all the nonsense, there really were some great insight, it would be completely useless if it is not part of the conversation.

You can tell from their letters that they aren't part of the conversation. They try to use the same words that scientists use, but they use them in ways that don't really mean what we mean, how we learned to use them in all those years we spent at University learning how to converse in the language of science.

It is exactly the same thing that happens to people who think they can find God without organized religion. They use ideas and words that they read someplace—probably in books produced by the very religions they are rejecting—without really understanding what they mean. They think they have grand insights into the nature of God and the Universe. But they are not in conversation with the rest of us...and by "us" I don't mean just with those of us around today, but with those of us who have lived in the past, who make up our traditions and history. They don't have referees to warn them when they're making mistakes. They wind up wallowing in a dream world devised by their own egos, rather than confronting the glorious but challenging and always slightly incomprehensible reality that true religion, and true science, tries to deal with.

And sometimes they do actually get it right. Johannes Kepler was such a person, someone with a very strange theology. Like the medievals, he thought that the physical universe should exactly mirror the nature of God. Since the Sun was the brightest thing in the sky, he assumed that it must represent the place of God the Father. The light coming off the Sun, he said, was the Holy Spirit. The realm of Earth on which it fell, was the same as the Second Person of the Trinity.

This really odd theology wasn't made any better by the fact that Kepler wrote in a terribly tortured form of Latin that many people had a hard time understanding. When he sent his books to Galileo, Galileo tossed them aside and never bothered to read them; he never even bothered to send Kepler a nice note of thanks. Frankly, in Galileo's place I would have done the same thing.

Because Kepler insisted that the Sun was like God, he also insisted that it must be the exact center of the universe. And he had read Copernicus deeply enough to realize that in the Copernican system, with perfectly circular orbits, the Sun actually had to move in a tiny circle around the center in order to make the positions of it and the other planets match the observations. This little eccentric circle, which most people hadn't noticed (I suspect they only looked at the pictures in Copernicus's book, and never actually read the math) was horrifying to Kepler. God the Father wouldn't make such a goofy little dance around nothing. So instead Kepler devised a system where the planets moved in ellipses, with the Sun fixed at a focus of the ellipse. It was only fifty years later that Edmund Halley, of comet fame, pointed out Kepler's work to Isaac Newton. Newton showed that his new theory of gravity actually predicted such elliptical orbits. Modern physics was finally born.

Kepler's theological idea was crazy. But it led to a scientific idea that was brilliant.

Meanwhile, Newton's successful physics led to its own odd development in the realm of science and religion. By being able to predict the positions and orbits of the planets with great accuracy, at least as accurate as people could observe back then, his physics gained great credibility. As the famous poem of Alexander Pope put it, "Nature and Nature's laws lay hid in night: God said, 'Let Newton be!' and all was light." And so people began to think that they could use the certainties of Newton's physics as a basis of religion. For example, there were many subtle points of planetary motions that Newton's physics couldn't exactly explain, at least not at first; surely these gaps were the places that proved God was necessary? Hence Newton's laws proved God's existence.

Of course we know what happens with this way of thinking. First, you reduce God to the sort of Watchmaker of the Deists, someone who merely winds up the Universe and lets it run, adjusting it as necessary from time to time. Then, you realize that all the gaps, all the adjustments you thought proved that you needed God, actually can be filled in with more subtle mathematics, without resorting to God after all. Your reason for believing in God gets squeezed out as the gaps get closed. Pretty soon you're an atheist who believes in a completely mechanical universe. (And then, of course, modern physics comes along and shows that all of Newton's assertions about the universe were terrible oversimplifications. Quantum physics gives a whole new set of gaps to lure us into thinking once again that we have science proving a need for God.)

Notice how in Galileo, Kepler, and Newton we find three different ways that people have tried to fit together faith and science.

Newton and his followers thought you could use science to prove the existence of God. Of course, the God they came up with was no longer the God of love, the God of scripture; and it eventually led to no God at all.

Kepler did the opposite; he thought that he could use his theology, his idea of God, as a basis for explaining how the universe ought to work. We honor Kepler today only because he was lucky enough to have come up with a description of orbits that worked, even though the philosophy it was based on it was total nonsense.

Galileo himself spoke of two separate ways to reach God, what he called "two books:" the book of scripture and the book of nature. (I remind you that Galileo, even after his terrible and unfair trial, remained a devout Catholic; his two daughters were both nuns.) But a lot of people have taken his "two books" idea as if they were separate ways to view the universe, without any overlap. You do science during the week, they say, and you leave religion to Sundays.

None of those ways work.

Father Michael Buckley, a Jesuit theologian, writes about this in *Denying and Disclosing God*. In the last chapter of his book, he points out that all of these attempts at connecting science and faith fail because they miss out on the essential fact of why we believe.

*Science and Faith Overlap in Human Beings*
*who Choose to do Science*

We are all scientists now, living in this scientific age; we all look for evidence for everything. And our theories (or theologies) are the way we organize what we believe in order to explain that evidence. What is the evidence on which we base our faith? It is not the orbits of the planets, or the position of the Sun or the Moon. It is not the authority of ancient sages, either saints or scientists. Instead, Buckley quotes a twentieth century philosopher, Raïssa Maritain, who came to Christianity by encountering, in history and in her life, the lives of saints. The essential data point for her was what she called "the fact of sanctity." Holiness exists. Any theory of the universe that fails to take into account that existence, is incomplete.

This can lead us to a deeper connection between faith and science. It is clear, I hope, that you cannot substitute one for the other; science does not replace faith, nor does faith replace science. And yet they do not deal with totally separate realms, as if they never overlap.

The fact is, science and religion do overlap most surely in one important place: in the human being who chooses to do the science, in the human being who comes to know the Creator through the things that have been Created.

Not every culture has produced scientists; not every religion supports science. And by support I don't just mean finding someone to pay your salary, though of course that's important; it is also the support of your family and friends, so your mom doesn't keep asking you why you're wasting your time doing science instead of making real money writing computer games.

Indeed there are three very important religious assumptions you have to make before you can do science.

The first assumption is that you must take on faith the proposition that the universe really exists. What we see is not mere illusion. We are not butterflies dreaming that we are scientists. There are some religious traditions and some philosophies who insist otherwise. One school of Zen insists that "all is illusion." Solipsism suggests that everything you experience is merely a projection of your own imagination...at least, that's what they claim, though I find it hard to imagine how you actually live this way from day to day. The humorous Irish writer George Bernard Shaw relates the story of confronting a woman who told him, "I am a solipsist, and so are most of my friends!"

The second assumption that you must make about the universe before you do any science on it is to accept on faith that there actually are scientific laws to be discovered, that effects have causes, that things don't just happen on a whim or at random. It seems obvious to us that scientific laws exist, because we have learned some of them and we can see that they work; but what gave the first scientists the confidence to think that there actually were such laws to be found?

If you were a believer in the ancient Roman gods, then when lightning struck you could blame Jupiter, god of lightning; when your crops grew well you could thank Ceres, goddess of crops. No need to look any further for why these things happened. When Christians came along they were persecuted for being atheists, and rightly so—they rejected all these nature gods in favor of one, supernatural, God. But if there are no nature gods, then you are free to speculate why natural events actually do occur.

There is a third and most subtle religious belief you must have before you can be a scientist, however…a belief that a lot of people today don't have. You must believe that science is worthy of spending your life doing. I don't mean making nice technological toys, like smart phones and iPods. Those are lovely, but that's a different level from doing the frankly useless work of trying to understand black holes or Martian weather. Pure science like astronomy won't make you rich, and it won't make you powerful—it's rather telling that you find astrologers and other fortune tellers in the poorer parts of town. It doesn't necessarily attract girls—at least it didn't for me! So why would anyone spend their life doing astronomy?

Worse yet, if you believe that the physical universe is fundamentally evil, a trap and a snare to pull you down from the more noble spiritual things of life, then your religion will actively try to stop you from wallowing in this dirty, dangerous physical morass. I remember once talking to a student from such a religion who wanted to become a geologist, but he was afraid—he asked me, "what will I tell my mom?"

By contrast, Christianity, Judaism, and Islam all teach of a universe that was deliberately created by a Creator God, who made things in an orderly way, step by step, and at each step of the way stopped to see that "It Was Good."

Even more, as Christians we believe that God so loved the world that He gave His Only Son for its redemption. As Saint Athanasius put it 1700 years ago in his book *On the Incarnation,* we are "cleansed and quickened" by the Incarnation of God into Nature that we celebrate during the Christmas season. And as he further states, the fact that the Word of God entered our world because He provided the works of creation as a means by which the Creator might be known. In that, Athanasius is only echoing St. Paul's letter to the Romans where in Chapter One he reminds us that from the beginning of time God has revealed Himself to us in the things that He has made.

We study creation to come closer to the Creator. And how do we know when we have come close to God? One sign is a sense of joy; a joy that I know I have felt when I encountered some wonderful insight into how the universe works. I don't mean just my own discoveries—those are few and far between—but other peoples' discoveries as well, which fill me with delight and a feeling of "rightness" in seeing how the pieces fit together, which is unmistakable once it has been experienced.

Learning to recognize those moments of rightness, those moments of God's presence, is another connection between science and faith. Science gives us experience with learning how to recognize the truth, and this experience can be invaluable when we search for truth in other endeavors. Notice that I am not talking about the truths themselves, but the way that science tries to find these truths.

First, it is important to remember that science describes, it does not prove. And those descriptions are constantly open to improvement.

Say you walk into a room, flip the switch on the wall, and the light comes on. For you, that's "proof" enough that the switch controls the light. But in point of fact, it could just be a coincidence—someone else could have hit the real switch at exactly the same time. The more often your switch seems to work, the higher the confidence you have that you've really found the right switch; but you can never be 100% sure that it isn't just a remarkable string of coincidences. (Or that someone isn't just playing a joke on you.)

Scientists report their findings with statistics to show just how confident they are that their theories are really describing what they think they see. But that confidence, while it can be very high, is never perfect. Even if you're 99.9% sure you got it right, you can expect one time out of a thousand you'll have been fooled. Yet you never know ahead of time which case will be the exception. And with thousands and thousands of such theories and experiments, inevitably those exceptions will pop up. They are rare; but they happen. The history of science is littered with theories that were logical, well supported by experiment, but nonetheless eventually found to be wrong.

But notice what that means about the attitude that a good scientist has to have. First of all, you have to admit you don't know everything; otherwise, you wouldn't be motivated to learn anything new. Secondly, you have to be humble enough to admit that, at any point along the way to new knowledge, you could go wrong. That's why you constantly test your ideas with experiments, and then test your experiments with better theories; why you work with others, rather than just work alone.

And that's why science books keep getting updated. While scientists rightly revere Galileo or Newton, nobody actually tries to learn astronomy or physics by reading their original books. As we make new discoveries, our understanding changes ("Pluto is not a planet!"). We find better ways of describing the things we've been looking at for centuries. By contrast, books of literature or philosophy—Plato, or Shakespeare, or the Bible—are timeless. Those books are not science books.

A religious believer can learn something from this humility. No matter how close to God we think we are, we must recognize that like his Creation, God too will always be more than we can ever completely know.

Science is always inadequate, always only partly true, always full of terrible oversimplifications. But we learn to recognize the pattern that truth makes; we develop a taste, an instinct, that helps us guess which theory of all the possible theories is the best one to pursue at this point, which possible experiment the next experiment I ought to try.

## Conclusion

It may sound funny to talk about guesses and instincts when dealing with the rational world of science, but the truth is that science is a wonderful blend of the rational with the instinctual. That is why science is not done by robots; it is done by human beings. Indeed, doing science is one of the things that makes us human.

I recall when I was a young postdoctoral fellow at MIT, before I joined the Jesuits, I would lie in bed late at night pondering the meaninglessness of my life. Why was I worried about the rings of Saturn when there were people starving in the world? Eventually I realized that I had no answer to that question. My life of a scientist was meaningless...or so I thought.

So I quit my job as a scientist and joined the US Peace Corps. I said I would go anywhere they sent me, do anything they asked me to do, as part of this big volunteer group working with the poor in the third world. They sent me to Africa, and told me I would be teaching high school science in a school up-country. But my assignment kept changing...a better high school, a government high school, a national high school...after three months I was assigned to the University of Nairobi, teaching postgraduate students, teaching astronomy.

There was a logic to it. To develop their nation, Kenya needed schools and teachers. The students I was teaching would go on to teach at the state Teacher's College to teach the teachers to teach the students, to raise the technical level of the nation.

But I would also go up-country, where the rest of my fellow volunteers were working, taking my small telescope with me, and in every village everyone would line up at night to see the rings of Saturn and the craters on the Moon. They were fascinated...exactly the same way as my friends and family back in America were fascinated to look at these things. And then finally it struck me: being in awe of the sky, looking at the nebulas in Orion and the galaxies in Andromeda, wondering about what it all is and how we fit into it, these are things that human beings do. I had a very clever cat in those days, but she never wanted to look through my telescope. Astronomy is something that makes us different from a cat, from well-fed cows.

And to deny someone the chance to indulge in those very human wonderings and longings, just because they were poor or hungry, is to deny them their humanity. Rather, to give them the opportunity to ponder these things is to feed their soul. And this is terribly important. The Africans taught me why we do astronomy, even in a world where people are hungry. One does not hunger for bread alone.

Both astronomy and religion remind us that there are bigger questions than "what's for dinner?" They force us out of our day to day concerns and see everything with a different perspective.

Perspective is what we learn from studying a trompe d'oeil dome like the one in St. Ignatius' Church that I mentioned earlier in this chapter. Perspective can fool us; or it can make us see things in a new way that we might not have realized before. If you walk around the church of St. Ignatius, look up at the ceiling, and see the "dome" from each of the wings of the building, you find that you have to be in just the right place to get the full effect of the artist's perspective. But if you look at it from a different place, you can appreciate how he did it.

Do we learn truth from science, or from religion? Which one gives us the truth? Like looking at that dome, you really only get the full truth when you have more than one point of view.

But, you might say, one point of view gives me an illusion, a lie! There is no dome, and one point of view is just fooling me into thinking that there's a dome. And that's true. If you only have one point of view you might well interpret what you see as something different from what it really is.

Yet here's an odd thing about illusion. Granted, that is not a real dome. But real domes do exist. And if you had never seen a real dome, if you did not know what a real dome was, if there were in fact no real domes, then this illusion wouldn't work at all. You wouldn't know what it is you were supposed to be seeing. You wouldn't be reminded of domes you have seen in the past. Your mind wouldn't be able to be led to the vision that the artist, Pozzo, painted; the vision that the architect, poor Father Grassi, had designed but which, for technical reasons, he couldn't complete. The illusion only works because of the reality that the illusion is attempting to invoke.

All our scientific descriptions of nature are, ultimately, illusions. They are incomplete. They are sketches; they are idealizations of the real thing; they are not "literally true." After all, even an equation in physics is a metaphor for the activity it describes; and a good mathematical physicist can read those metaphors like a poem. They are not themselves the truth. But they point us to the truth.

And likewise all our descriptions of God can only be poetry; no mere words can describe that which is beyond description. But like that painting on the ceiling, a good piece of art—and science is ultimately a masterful piece of human art—can lead our imaginations beyond our mortal bounds into realms that we can only now glimpse from afar.

I am a scientist and I am a Jesuit brother. But you can't split me in two and say this part is the man of science, that part is the man of faith, any more than you could split Grassi into the mathematician or the astronomer or the architect, any more than you can split the painting of the dome into what it looks like from one point of view versus what it looks like from someplace else, to say that sometimes it is a dome but other times some strange abstract shape. Both are the one and same painting on the ceiling.

It is the one same universe that we live in, scientist and believer, and the one same truth we search for. If we are both observer and believer, we are blessed in being able to look at that truth from more than one direction and thus learn things that one direction alone could never tell us.

And we are all called to be scientists in that way. We may not all learn the language of science, the poetry of the mathematics, or participate daily in the conversation. But you don't have to be a musician to listen to music. You don't have to be a saint yourself to observe the sanctity of others. You don't have to be an artist to appreciate painting. I can't paint perspective like Brother Pozzo but I can let his talent pull me up into his vision of an infinity over my head.

We have been given the gift of intelligence to at least look through the telescope and be amazed by the beauty of nebulae and rings. We all have been given the ability to know other people and experience God's presence within them. It just requires us to open our eyes and see.

That is the faith of a scientist.

# 2

# Notes on the History of the Dialectic between Scientific and Humanistic Knowing

## Sergio Rondinara

I N THE MIDDLE AGES, culture in general was strongly characterized by a theologically-informed way of reasoning. In
the seventeenth century, however, there was a shift to something quite different. Two important events characterized this
shift. Firstly, a gradual separation of theological and philosophical reasoning took place. Secondly, the modern natural sciences emerged and they were distinct from the realm of natural
philosophy. The emergence in this period of modern scientific
reasoning consisted in what we could call a new conceptual
space, capable of producing a form of knowledge that was new
compared to what had previously been commonly accepted.

Galileo Galilei (1564–1642), in his letter to Mark Welser of
December 1, 1612, while discussing sunspots, was the first to
express awareness of this newness:

> Either we want to try to penetrate the true and intrinsic es-
> sence of natural substances through speculation, or we want
> to content ourselves with some general knowledge of their
> effects. Trying for the essence is, according to me, not less
> impossible and—as far as our effort is concerned—not less
> vain when it is directed towards the elemental substances as
> for those which are most remote and celestial.[1]

---

1.   G. Galilei, *Lettera a Marco Velseri* (December 1, 1612), in Id., *Le opere di Galileo Galilei*, edited by A. Favaro (Florence: Barbèra Publishing Company, 1932), vol. V, pp. 187–188. It should be noted that Italian texts in this article have been translated by Declan O'Byrne, Sophia University Institute.

Galileo believed that there was an intrinsic weakness in the way of research that had been followed previously in that it wanted to investigate "essence", an objective that he considered too ambitious. He rejected this way and focused on a more limited and apparently less ambitious objective, namely that of knowing "some of the effects" of natural objects, or—as we might say today—of trying to describe with precision the features of natural phenomena.

With Galileo's decision we see a move away from an investigation of essences, that up to that point had been considered the primary task of philosophy (understood as well-founded knowledge, *episteme*), and the beginning of a non-philosophical knowledge of nature, a knowledge that no longer had the goal of discovering natural essences, their causes and the principles that determine them, but rather of explaining the relation between phenomena.

This new form of knowledge represented a methodological revolution, the fruit of centuries of philosophical development. It was no longer simply based on the simple deductive reasoning of formal logic, but rather on a fruitful collaboration between the senses and the intellect, between empirical observation and the mathematical expression of experience. These, as Galileo put it, were "sense experiences"[2] and "necessary demonstrations".[3]

This new direction in the form of knowing didn't immediately catch on in universities. In the eyes of both Aristotelian and non-Aristotelian university professors of the time, it seemed like an utter renunciation of all true knowledge of the secrets of nature. However it took only a few decades to bring about a new image of the natural and human world, giving rise to a new type of intellectual, and also to new types of institutions beyond the university environment such as scientific academies and societies.[4]

---

2. By "sense experiences" is meant the observational or experimental observation of natural phenomena, appropriately abstracted from their environment, to facilitate their study. These observations or experiments were designed to be measurable through instruments.

3. The "necessary demonstrations" were those arguments based no longer on logical syllogistic deductions, but on the application of geometry and mathematics to the products of observation and experiment.

4. In Rome, for instance, in 1603 the Accademia dei Lincei was established

Initially, this new form of knowing was presented in the academic world as a form of knowing that was open to the study of the Humanities which were essentially philosophical and theological. However, on the basis of the autonomy of its method, the newly born science tried to establish itself as a field of knowledge that was free from those bonds of authority to be found in the philosophical tradition then predominant in the universities. It proclaimed itself as having nothing in common with theological learning. It wanted to establish its autonomy from philosophy and theology while at the same time presenting itself as a knowledge that, once its autonomy had been recognized, would remain open to relations with these two important forms of human knowledge. It did not give signs of wishing to oppose or substitute either of them.

It is precisely this attempt to establish itself as an open form of knowledge, capable of defending its own methodological autonomy in relation to philosophy and theology that gave rise to the dialectic between forms of knowledge that has characterized and continues to characterize European culture. In this paper, I will attempt to present briefly some of the historical developments and key theoretical insights of this dialectic.

## 1. The Seventeenth Century: The Dramatic Dawn

By concentrating on quantitative rather than qualitative analysis of natural phenomena,[5] the newborn science highlighted the mutual correlation between *sense experience* and *necessary demonstrations*. Thanks to its success it began to be recognized as a new and authentic form of knowledge. As well as that, among natural philosophers of the time it was widely believed that the structure of the physical world was characterized by mathematical order,[6] and that therefore one could describe natural phenomena in mathematical terms. This strongly characterized

---

through the work of prince Federico Cesi. In 1645, in London, the Royal Society for the Promotion of Natural Knowledge was founded. In 1657 in Florence, the Accademia del Cimento was created. And in 1666, the Académie royale des sciences was born in Paris. These were places in which those practicing the new field of knowledge—professors, experimenters and craftsmen as well as students—met together for discussion and the publication of their works.

5. Galileo, for example, denied the reality of sensible realities, regarding these as simply subjective impressions of the senses. See G. Galilei, *Il saggiatore*, in Id., *Le opere*, op. cit., vol. VI, pp. 347–348.

6. See G. Galilei, *Il Saggiatore*, in Id., *Le opere*, cit., vol. VI, p. 232.

the methodology of the newborn science as a study that was independent of traditional natural philosophy, and yet also capable of explaining natural reality and therefore of offering true judgements about it.

Because of the development of this new and original methodology, scientific thought soon began to set aside traditional metaphysical axioms and then, in order to gain its own autonomy, to free itself entirely from them. Some noted figures active in this period preferred, however, to continue a philosophical kind of research into nature. For instance, René Descartes (1596–1650), used mathematics in his metaphysics of nature to provide an absolute picture of the physical world whose essence he identified as a *res extensa* (corporeal substance) underlying movement.

A similar approach to knowledge, one that was purely theoretical and deductive, was passed on by Descartes to some Dutch scientists such as Christian Huygens (1596–1687). In doing this, however, awareness of the limits of scientific research was lost, since the expectation that natural phenomena should receive a mechanical explanation was already a sign that the methodological caution of the newborn science was being abandoned, and that science was now positioning itself within a mechanistic prospective. Other scientists and philosophers accepted the Galilean distinction between science and philosophy.

Gottfried Leibniz (1646–1716) proposed a distinction between science and philosophy based on the different kinds of problems that the two disciplines face. Questions belonging to philosophy included those dealing with final cause. Scientific questions, however, are dominated by the search for necessary causes. Given this rather subtle distinction, Liebniz viewed science and philosophy as distinct due to the manner in which reality is examined. Leibniz rejected Descartes' pure deductive method—reducing physics to mathematics—but appreciated the mathematical formulation of experience itself. He also recognized that the physical world is not, as in the deductive method, the realm of necessary conclusions deriving from the principle of non-contradiction, and that it is enough to assign "sufficient reasons" for phenomena.

Among the scientists who accepted the Galilean distinction between science and philosophy, we should certainly list Isaac Newton (1642–1727). He explicitly declared this in the beginning of his fundamental work *Philosophiae Naturalis Principia Mathematica*, where from the very first lines he specified the kind of philosophy that he wanted to develop:

> Since the ancients held the science of *mechanics* in the highest consideration in the investigation of natural things, and the moderns having rejected substantial forms and occult qualities, have tried to reduce natural phenomena to mathematical laws, it seemed opportune in this tractate to cultivate *mathematics* for that part that belonged to philosophy.[7]

We can clearly see here Newton's intention to follow the Galilean way with regard to the search for essences (indicated by the term "substantial forms"). What is interesting in Newton, however, are the considerations he presented on the last page of the General Scholium with which he concludes the work. After having presented in his tractate the three principles of dynamics and the law of universal gravitation, Newton poses the question about what is gravity, and what its essence is. In that context, he affirms:

> In truth, I have not yet managed to deduce from the phenomena the cause of these properties of gravity, and I will not invent hypotheses.[8] Whatever is not deducible from the phenomena should be called *hypotheses*, and in experimental philosophy there is no room for hypotheses whether metaphysical or physical, whether occult or mechanical.[9]

When Newton speaks here of hypotheses, he is not referring to the field of scientific hypotheses (he himself was a master of formulating and proving such hypotheses), but rather to uncontrollable metaphysical hypotheses and conjectures. He declares that he does not want to invent *ad hoc* hypotheses to explain what could not be explained scientifically. His position is very clear—everything beyond scientific endeavours (such as metaphysical propositions) were to be rigorously excluded from science.

---

7.   I. Newton, *Principi matematici della filosofia naturale*, (Turin: Utet, 1989), p. 57.
8.   In the original Latin: hypotheses non fingo.
9.   I. Newton, *Principi matematici della filosofia naturale*, cit., pp. 801–802.

For Newton, gravity really exists, and offers a satisfactory explanation for the movement of bodies and allows us to predict their future positions, and that is enough for Newton, the experimental philosopher (i.e. physicist). However much they might continue to interest Newton the man, for him questions about the reasons for gravity or the essence of gravity went beyond the realm of experimental philosophy.

It is interesting to note how the Galilean way of not looking for essences leads Newton to the first true paradigm[10] of modern physics that, on the one hand, will give rise to remarkable results in the understanding of the movement of heavenly bodies, unprecedented in the history of humanity, but that, at the same time, leaves untouched the metaphysical question of what gravity is. The fact that this latter question remains open attests to the openness of scientific thought to philosophy and to the fact that science does not at this stage claim to be a totalizing or all-encompassing way of knowledge. It is a form of knowledge that, once it has reached its objectives, calls upon the human intellect to move beyond science, no longer as a scientist, but as a human being, to face broader and more complex questions than those science itself examines, and to carry scientific knowing along interdisciplinary paths towards an interaction between various fields of human enquiry.

The metaphysical question itself attests to the value of a healthy distinction between scientific reason and philosophical reason, between science and philosophy. After Newton, however, this distinction fell ever more by the wayside, giving way firstly to balancing the two forms of knowledge and then to their mutual indifference.

Regarding method, Newton was aware of the centrality of experience, to the point of holding — under the influence of the empiricists — that experience alone is capable of giving the enquirer an adequate knowledge about physical reality. Unlike his contemporary Leibniz, in his reflections on method Isaac Newton appears not to recognize the Galilean dialectic between

---

10. Newtonian physics presents the universe as consisting of separated corpuscles or particles which interact through a hypothetical distance action within an absolute and empty space (existing in itself and independent from every kind of material), and in the flowing of an absolute universal time (also existing in itself and independent of the movement of bodies).

induction and deduction (though that oversight is not absent from his actual praxis as scientist).

All of this shows the gradual manner in which the conceptual developments proposed by Galileo regarding modern scientific rationality were received into the tradition. In the authors we have just cited, even if the terms *science* and *philosophy* do not appear (in this period science and philosophy were still considered as synonymous), an awareness gradually develops that they are two different modes of knowing reality. As I mentioned earlier, all of this takes place in scientific academies and societies, i.e. outside the universities.

Even at this early stage, the relationship between science and theology was characterized by a number of difficulties. In terms of the interaction between science and theology, both for scientists and for theologians a point that seemed to need to be defended was the revealed message of the Bible. The problem that emerged was that of seeing whether the "profane" cultural contents, such as the Copernican doctrine, could be harmonized with the biblical message or whether at times these doctrines led to distortions of the Christian faith. The Galileo case demonstrates this clearly. Both the scientist from Pisa and his inquisitors realized that the central problem was that of Scripture. There was no disagreement about the need to reach an understanding between the doctrines of Scripture and the new science. The difficulty related to how this understanding was to be reached and what were the limits of the autonomy that could be conceded to scientific research.

In letters, firstly to Father Benedetto Castelli[11] and, secondly to the Grand Duchess Christina di Lorena,[12] Galileo proposed an interpretation of Scripture that would protect the absolute truth of the scriptural text and the truth discovered by scientific research. He set out the principle that the Bible should not be used for gaining knowledge of natural phenomena, the Bible being based on a common pre-scientific knowledge of natural events. The problem was thus related not so much to the separation of two fields of knowledge, but rather, as we might

---

11.   G. Galilei, *Lettera a D. Benedetto Castelli*, in Id. *Le opere*, op. cit., vol. V, pp. 279–288.
12.   G. Galilei, *Lettera a Madama Cristina di Lorena*, op. cit., vol. V, pp. 309–348.

say today, the issue of theological epistemology and in particular of biblical hermeneutics.

In his attempt to affirm the undoubted authority of the Bible in the fields of faith and morals, and at the same time defending the legitimacy of the newborn scientific discourse understood as an interpretation of the *book of nature*[13] that has God as its author, Galileo proposed (in vain) the incommensurability of scientific and theological knowledge. Such incommensurability meant, on the one hand, that the two discourses could not contradict one another while being, on the other hand, compatible as different expressions of human knowledge.

The establishment of a new methodology led to the gradual development of the newborn science. On the philosophical level this development was undoubtedly favored by currents like empiricism and Cartesian rationalism. These offered a philosophical grounding of the new science that was *in contrast* to other currents of thought such as Aristotelianism that by this time were generally judged incapable of expressing a true understanding of nature. Subsequently, however, the fracture caused by the bitter fallout from the Galileo case, together with the developments of the Cartesian philosophy, meant that rationalism and philosophical materialism came to have greater influence on European culture than the philosophy that had developed within the Christian tradition. This led to an ever greater divergence between scientific knowledge and critical knowledge of faith.

In the seventeenth century, Johannes Kepler (1571–1630), a young German astronomer working in the court of Prague, viewed his program of metaphysical research as consisting of a search for God's signature in the cosmos: "...the universe is the Book of Nature in which the Creator God, in a writing without words, has revealed and explained his essence as well as what he wants of human beings."[14] It makes a strong impression on us today to hear such words from the scientist who was the first to identify the three laws of planetary motion. In Kepler,

---

13. Cf. G. Galilei, *Lettera a Elia Diodati*, in Id. *Le opere*, op. cit., vol. XV, p. 25; Id., *Lettera a D. Benedetto Castelli*, op. cit., vol. V, pp. 232–285; Id., *Il Saggiatore*, op. cit., p. 232.

14. J. Kepler, *Mysterium Cosmographicum, Praefatio*, in *Gesammelte Werke*, I, (Munich: Beck, 1938–75), p. 5.

religious thought is still entwined in a balanced way with scientific knowledge, as is demonstrated, for example, in the prayer of Book 5 of his *Harmonices Mundi*[15] in which we find cosmological affirmations strictly connected to Christological themes, or, to give another example, when at the conclusion of the same work he offers a doxological hymn to God, the Creator of the cosmos. For the German astronomer the study of nature supported his religious belief and the universe appeared to him as *cosmos* (ordered world). The three scientific laws that today carry his name were not considered by him as impersonal, nor was the universe that they regulated regarded as a casual product of their action. Rather, for Kepler, the universe was a carefully planned system, since "God does nothing by chance"[16] and he orders his creatures according to those mathematical principles that are coeternal with God himself.

Just a generation later, with René Descartes, we find the first cracks in the unity between Christian faith and science that we see in Kepler. In the French philosopher we find an attempt to reconcile Christian thought with the contributions of newborn science, giving an unconditional primacy however to science. Descartes' God is no longer the Triune God who creates and redeems the world out of love, but is rather the God of the philosophers, a God necessary for the maintenance of all beings in existence. Furthermore, in his cosmological synthesis, given the impossibility of knowing final causes, the divine goals of things, there is no trace of intelligent planning. For Descartes, God does not reveal himself through the structure of the universe. He reveals himself, rather, in the regularity of natural phenomena which we can learn of more through the study of the laws of nature than through the religious posture of adoration of a transcendent God.

## 2. Contrast with Philosophy and Disconnection from Religious Thought

A decisive step towards distinguishing science and philosophy on more than just terminological grounds is found in the work of Immanuel Kant (1724–1804). In his *Critique of Pure*

---

15. Cf. J. Kepler, *Gesammelte Werke*, op. cit., VI, p. 331.
16. J. Kepler, Letter to *Michael Maestlin* (2 August 1595), in *Gesammelte Werke*, op. cit., XIII, p. 27.

*Reason*, he examines the conditions of possibility according to which knowledge in the domain of reason may be pursued. For Kant the word "science" assumes once again the character of a knowledge distinguished by necessity, universality and system. He recognizes that disciplines like mathematics and physics had recently acquired the status of sciences, while metaphysics continued to be something remote. This gives rise to the first question of the first Critique: whether it is possible to have metaphysics as science.

What strikes us about Kant is that the term "science", even though it continues to have a generic meaning, shows a profound change in its usage. While prior to him, the model of scientific knowledge had been philosophy and especially metaphysics, with Kant we begin to see that it is mathematics and physics that exemplify scientific knowledge. Physics was now established on the firmer grounds indicated by Galileo and—for Kant—for the first time it could be considered the certain path of science: "To this single idea must the revolution be ascribed, by which, after groping in the dark for so many centuries, natural science was at length conducted into the path of certain progress."[17]

The importance of this development is due not just to the fact that soon thereafter the term "science" would be reserved exclusively for disciplines like physics and mathematics, but also because such a change—together with the results of the *Critique of Pure Reason* which seal the impossibility of doing metaphysics as *science*—establishes the custom of counterpoising science and religion. Science will be taken as authentic knowledge and philosophy will be the place of moral certainties, but philosophy will be deprived of any capacity to gain real knowledge. Why was there such a reversal of the model of scientific learning such that knowledge passed from philosophy to mathematical physics? Simply because in the 94 years that separated the publication of Newton's *Principia* (1687) and the *Critique of Pure Reason* (1781), physics and especially mechanics had developed so much in an autonomous manner and brought about such a series of successes that the weight of evidence in favor of that model was overwhelming. Already at this stage an

---

17. I. Kant, *Critique of Pure Reason*, translated by M. D. Meiklejohn (Penn University Electronic Classic Series), p. 12.

autonomous science of nature existed, apart from philosophical discussions, and was already preparing to enter the universities. It had become impossible to ignore this new and autonomous field of study.

In the eighteenth century, we see in Europe the complete separation of scientific and theological discourse. Thanks to its successes, science became increasingly sure of itself and aware of its heuristic capacities, that is enabling a person to discover or learn something for themselves. The greatest exponent of this process was, undoubtedly, Isaac Newton. It is true that in his published works we find various expressions of religious faith that recall traditional religious piety: these remain despite the strong development of scientific rationality evident in his work. On the other hand, if we examine his unpublished work regarding religious topics we discover an adult Newton intent on an intense critique of traditional religious views and clearly occupying a position of sincere theism stripped of the divinity of Christ.

In his *Theologiae Gentilis Origines Philosophicae*, considered the most important work for his heterodox theological opinions and drafted the year prior to *Philosophiae Naturalis Principia Mathematica*, the Cambridge scientist sees himself in a line that runs from Kepler to Descartes and conceives of nature as God's revelation, at least equal to the revelation found in the Bible, or perhaps greater. He distances himself significantly, however, from the Cartesian philosophy of nature, in which every physical being of nature was produced by the necessary activity of natural laws. Such a conception of the autonomy of the world in relation to God seemed to him too close to atheism. Though rejecting the academic Aristotelianism of his time, Newton unreservedly accepted the notion of final causality because he thought it the best argument for proving the existence of God. Beyond that he held that God continued his activity in creation and connected his immanence to the functioning of his laws. Newton did not, as a matter of fact, regard gravity—which he formulated in his *Principia* and which so wonderfully explained the movement of celestial bodies—as a property of matter itself, but rather held God himself to be the agent that continually operated on bodies making them move according to his laws.

Regarding the inhering of God and nature, Newton's position was essentially based on biblical revelation and on the Greek philosophy of Anaxagoras from whom he borrowed the concept of *perichoresis*.[18] He understood transcendence and immanence as related to one another through a free and mutual co-presence without any form of necessity for either of the two realities. Speaking of the Divinity, the great English scientist wrote the following in the *Principia*: "In it are contained and moved the universes. God suffers nothing due to the movement of bodies: these find no resistance on account of God's omnipotence."[19]

As far as Newton was concerned, his scientific interpretation of the sensible world was not a threat to faith, but it was the basis upon which his religious vision of the world was built. In the General Scholium at the end of the *Principia* we find discussion "about God: of whom natural philosophy is called to speak, taking phenomena as its starting point"[20]:

> The wonderful arrangement of the sun, the planets and comets could not have been born apart from the design and power of an intelligent and powerful Being. And if the fixed stars are at the centre of similar systems, all of these, being built according to the same design will also be subject to the power of the One [...]. And so that the systems of fixed stars do not fall in on one another due to gravity, the same Being placed an immense distance between them.[21]

For Newton theological reflection had such importance that he thought that this, more than his scientific work, would have been the aspect of his thought that would have had greater long-term influence.

Scientific reason with its great heuristic capacity — expressed in such an exemplary manner by Newton's own works — gained greater prominence during the Enlightenment, despite Kant's criticism that attempted a re-dimensioning of empirical knowledge. Eighteenth-century rationalism gave considerable impulse to what in nineteenth-century positivism

---

18. Anaxagoras was the first to introduce the term "perichoresis" to ancient philosophy, to indicate that every physical being contains in itself all other things, without becoming confused with them.
19. I. Newton, *Principi matematici della filosofia naturale*, op. cit., p. 800.
20. Ibid. p. 801.
21. Ibid. pp. 800–801.

would become the full independence of scientific thought. Symbolic of this further development is the well-known dialogue between the mathematician and astronomer Pierre Simon de Laplace (1749–1827) and Napoleon Bonaparte. When the French scientist expounded for the emperor the broad lines of his cosmological doctrine according to which the universe had its origins in an initial nebula, Napoleon asked him "What is the place of God in your system?" Laplace responded, "I have no need of that hypothesis." For Laplace, once the hypothesis of the existence of an initial nebula was accepted, it was enough to use the laws of Newtonian mechanics to describe the universe in its structure and so there was no need of other hypotheses.

In this phrase we can see the birth of a positivistic spirit in which God and the transcendent dimension are no longer considered within science. Laplace's response became the paradigmatic expression of an agnostic position within science and which as such was and is compatible with two diametrically opposed developments[22]: an *atheistic* development, in which the God hypothesis is viewed as useless not only as science, but as useless even for understanding the overall meaning of the cosmos; and the *theist* development in which the reality of God can be affirmed on extra-scientific grounds and is not just not in contrast with, but even in harmony with science. After this, on the philosophical plane, Auguste Comte's (1798–1857) laws of the *three stages* of humanity with the assertion that human development can be understood as moving from a *theological* (or false) stage to a *metaphysical* (or abstract) stage and thence to a *scientific* (or positive) stage—was the theoretical expression of what had already become a common way of thinking. This is how the complete separation expressed by Laplace between theological and scientific discourse deepened during the nineteenth century to the point of becoming real opposition.

## 3. Scientistic Mechanism in Opposition to Theology

The nineteenth century was to be the century in which we find science tempted to present itself as philosophy. Mechanism emerged strongly and scientific research moved quickly ahead on its own, increasingly distrustful of philosophy. For science

---

22. Cf. E. Agazzi, Scienza e fede. *Nuove prospettive su un vecchio problema*, Massimo, Milano 1983, p. 112.

this was also the century of the great theoretical syntheses in which the great bulk of knowledge that had been accumulated to that point was systematically framed in an array of theories capable of giving an explanation for everything.

It is in the nineteenth century that science mechanics gradually dominates. Mechanistic language is used more. Terms such as mass and force, space and velocity are used to describe the most disparate phenomena of nature including those not affected by gravitational phenomenology such as electrics, magnetism and thermal physics. This led to the proposal of mechanics as the interpretative key for physical reality, a key that was of a basically philosophical kind. The mechanism of the nineteenth century, unlike that of the seventeenth century, presented itself as an attempt to explain the whole physical universe in mechanical terms, and so we find an extrapolation from physical mechanics into the philosophical field.

Mechanics came to be more than a science, it came to be a *scientific conception of the world*: mechanism as philosophy. Modern science, born in the seventeenth century with the precise intention of not seeking the "essences" of things and of limiting itself to the investigation of phenomena, reneged on its origins and took on to itself the burden of offering absolute affirmations regarding the essence of physical things just like the Aristotelian physics that it had criticized two centuries previously.

An echo of this state of affairs was found in philosophy itself with the rise of positivism, whose principal meaning was that of legitimizing the philosophical claims of science and attributing to it competence not only over the investigation of nature, but even over the entire field of human problems, thus declaring science the only authentic form of knowledge capable of facing and resolving this whole range of problems. Scientism was born.

The elevation of physics to the rank of philosophy was undoubtedly an exciting experience for the world of science, but it was not to last for long, and eventually led to disappointment. The presuppositions for the dissolution of mechanism as the interpretative key for all reality were already to be found in its reductionistic operations aimed at explaining phenomena that exceeded in complexity those classically and successfully dealt with by mechanics. As a matter of fact, mechanism was compromised from within wherever its attempts to dominate all physical phenomena had been most daring.

Some of the more methodologically careful scientists were aware that mechanistic schemes could not hope to give an authentic picture of the constitution of the world, but could only offer models to explain certain phenomena. Thus, for example, we see the emergence of the English school that explored the use of models. We can think of scientists of the calibre of Faraday, Thomson, and Maxwell.

One of those encouraging the recovery of such methodological caution was undoubtedly Heinrich Rudolf Hertz (1857–1894), who in his *Principles of Mechanics* (1876)[23] affirmed that physics makes affirmations in limited sectors of nature, and that therefore it had limited validity. He also affirmed the thesis according to which physics is not philosophy and therefore does not have the task of offering a complete picture of nature, but only of offering images of phenomena.

The first half of the nineteenth century was a most significant phase in the institutional history of natural sciences. In this period science makes its entry into the universities. This event took place on a grand scale, firstly in central Europe in nations such as Germany, Poland, the Netherlands, Scandinavia, in the Czech lands, Switzerland, Austria and Hungary,[24] and while in France the same movement took place, it was on a less grand scale. The process of inclusion of science in the universities in the United Kingdom and in the United States of America took place a few decades later, largely inspired by the Germanic model. With this entry into the universities, modern science assumed a professional and institutional role in society.

Regarding the relationship between science and theological learning, in the nineteenth century we pass from the separation of science and theology to a situation of tension between them. Nineteenth-century positivism didn't just raise scientific knowledge to the highest level of human knowledge, but also held — ignoring every methodological limit intrinsic to scientific research — that scientific reason was the "model" form of

---

23. H.R. Hertz, *Die Prinzipien der Mechanik* (Leipzig 1894).
24. See Cf. J. Ben-David, *The Scientist's Role in Society* (Prentice-Hall, Englewood Cliffs (N.J.) 1971).

knowledge against which every other kind of human knowledge should be measured. The exponents of scientific reason defended the primacy of scientific knowledge over metaphysical and theological knowledge as the only valid method for a true knowledge. For them, the method of natural sciences should be extended also to study of social sciences, since sociology was regarded as the part of the philosophy of nature that concentrated on social phenomena.

This was the period in which scientism flourished and was the cultural context in which Charles Darwin's (1809–1882) theory of biological evolution developed. Darwin was attempting to compose an overall picture of the multiplicity of living beings in the biosphere. On the cultural level he brought about a naturalistic reading of the entirety of reality. To the ancient but ever new question of human origins, the evolutionary conception responded that it was enough to go back through the data that illustrate the rise of biological, chemical and physical phenomena from which the phenomenon of life emerged. All of this could be very well realized without any reference to the creative acts of a transcendent God.

This meant that the human being was derived from a previously existing natural being, through biological processes, regulated by chance variations and natural selection, and that even his moral and intellectual qualities were no more than the further specialization of certain features already present in animals that preceded him on the evolutionary ladder. Such positions represented serious threats to the religious convictions of the time and appeared as a falsification of the biblical accounts of creation and gave no account of a divine plan since the above mentioned evolutionary variations were the fruit of chance and not of a plan.

Darwin's scientific theory fed into and sustained a true vision of the world for the culture of the time, with its totalizing vision characterized by the rejection of the principle of creation and by an a-teleological view of nature called "evolutionism". For a long time this ideological position came to be the foundation of scientific atheism and opposed all theological and philosophical efforts to think of "God" as a necessary subject for the explanation of the origin of humanity. If, for Laplace, God had become an unnecessary hypothesis for the explanation of natural phenomena, with evolutionism God and the notion of creation become a clumsy hypothesis to be excluded from our horizon of ideas. The separation, as we see in Laplace, between theological and scientific affirmations about the same physical reality soon developed, on account of evolutionism, into opposition. The reactions of theology and of the churches were immediate, harsh and clearly directed towards an irreconcilability of scientific and faith affirmations. Scientific affirmations were contrary to the Christian tradition, while the affirmations of faith were held to be foundational for an authentic understanding of human reality. The clear contrast between the dynamic naturalistic vision nourished by Darwinian evolutionism and the static and fixed religious creationist conception, fed into the sustained polemics and the climate of conflict in the entire Christian West, and carried on in different phases right up until the final years of the twentieth century.[25]

## 4. Indifference and the Decline of Opposition

In the twentieth century the logical positivism of the Vienna Circle attempted to promote a unified science capable of containing in itself all human knowledge about reality through the use of logic. Moving beyond the balancing attempted by previous generations there's an attempt now to eliminate all metaphysical affirmations about God and the transcendent from the realm of real knowledge. Such affirmations are now understood as simply meaningless. This position led the scientific culture to attack the religious sphere both as true knowledge and on the practical level, causing profound wounds in the contemporary religious consciousness. Scientism seriously impugned the conceptual space of transcendence to the point of rendering it difficult for contemporary culture to perceive the transcendent.

The twentieth century was, however, also a time that began to see the decline of hardened positions promoting opposition between science and religion. This decline was motivated by changes in both fields.

In the scientific realm there's a gradual dismantling of scientism and its overblown conception of scientific reason. The

---

25. Cf. C. Molari, *Darwinismo e teologia cattolica*, Rome: Borla, 1994.

birth during the early decades of the century of quantum mechanics which, also along with Werner Heisenberg's (1901–1976) uncertainty principle[26] forced physicists to determine the movement of elementary particles through probability calculations—represented the first serious blow to rigid Laplacian determinism according to which the future history of a given physical system was univocally determined by the knowledge of the initial conditions and of the scientific laws that regulated the development of the system.

A few years later, in 1931, another key idea of scientism, namely the belief that only science possessed the appropriate language for the description of reality was cancelled by the formulation in formal logic of the Incompleteness Theorem[27] by Kurt Gödel (1906–1978). According to this theorem, in a system of axioms, containing a system of whole numbers, there exist statements that cannot be demonstrable. This theorem when applied to our theme affirms that a given scientific theory does not have in itself the proof of its own coherence.

A third bastion of scientism to collapse was that according to which in order to define a given physical system it is enough to know the elements that make it up. This is the position that generates ontological reductionism according to which the complex can be reduced to the elementary, to the simple. This position disappeared with the birth of complex systems theory[28] and the development of information theory. It is now held that new information can appear in a given physical system that does not belong to the elements of the system when the elements that compose it are in the condition to become a system. It has also been recognized that the observer has an essential role in identifying the nature of physical reality, and that faced with the numerous conquests of science it almost always becomes necessary to redefine the concepts of space, time, matter, evolution, life etc. All of this has had the effect of making scientists

---

26. W. Heisenberg, Über den anschaulichen Inhalt der quantentheoretischen Kinematik und Mechanik, in *Zeitschrift für Physik*, 43 (1927) pp. 172–198.

27. K. Gödel, Über formal unentscheidbare Säze der Principia Mathematica und verwandter Systeme I, in *Monatshefte für Mathematik und Physik*, 38 (1931) pp. 173–178.

28. Cf., R.J. Russell - N. Murphy - A.R. Peacocke (Eds.), *Chaos and Complexity. Scientific Perspectives on Divine Action*, Vatican Observatory, Vatican City State 1995.

more open to other forms of knowledge, and less certain about the possibility of achieving irreversible knowledge of the world. These changes have contributed to the spread of a more cautious tone in the treatment of the relations between science and theology compared to how these were approached in the past.

There have also been developments in theology. Modern interpretations of scripture showed themselves willing to leave behind fixed descriptions of the cosmos and, more generally, the claim of finding elements that would reinforce religious belief in the scientific study of origins. In Catholic theology, this process has been encouraged by a renewed theology of faith, strictly related to a renewed theology of revelation. Thanks to biblical and historical research, not to mention ecumenical dialogue, theology has promoted a broader notion of revelation than simply the supernatural communication of certain truths inaccessible to humans or unreachable because of the situation of sin in which we live. We see the new paradigm of Revelation presented by the Second Vatican Council in its Dogmatic Constitution on Divine Revelation: *Dei Verbum*.

In the Catholic church, the new position regarding the relations of theology and science was expressed in another important text of the Second Vatican Council, *Gaudium et spes*, in those passages where it refers to the autonomy of terrestrial realities:

> [...] if methodical investigation within every branch of learning is carried out in a genuinely scientific manner and in accord with moral norms, it never truly conflicts with faith, for earthly matters and the concerns of faith derive from the same God. [...] We cannot but deplore certain habits of mind, which are sometimes found among Christians, which do not sufficiently attend to the rightful independence of science and which, from the arguments and controversies they spark, lead many minds to conclude that faith and science are mutually opposed.[29]

Subsequently, the church, and especially Pope John Paul II in many important interventions, has given a strong push within the Catholic environment towards greater dialogue between theology and the natural sciences. This new attitude goes

---

29. Second Vatican Council, *Gaudium et spes*, n. 36.

far beyond the polemical antagonism towards the sciences and the denunciations of atheism that had characterized the past.

Within philosophy during the last 80 years important progress has been made in the area of the philosophy of science. In place of the verificationist position of logical positivism found at the beginning of the century,[30] we have seen the rise of Popper's falsification criterion,[31] which then too had to be revised in the light of the historical-social revolution launched in the sixties by Thomas Kuhn (1922–1996).[32] The debate which followed between followers of Popper and Kuhn[33] threw new light on the process of scientific knowledge and directed the development of reflection on the sciences of the last three decades up to the current debate between instrumentalists and realists.[34]

The image of science that has emerged from this long process is that of a methodologically controlled cognitive adventure that has the goal of knowing the structure and history of the natural world. The physical beings of the world, to the extent that they are physical, and the natural phenomena that are the object of sense experience, are the object of study for the natural sciences, and the method with which they proceed is that of the formation of programs of scientific research. These programs enter into competition with one another and, in the critical phase of competition, can substitute one another in what are truly scientific revolutions.

For many scientists, these epistemological acquisitions have meant recognizing the need for greater conceptual and mental elasticity, the need to recognize the value of the diverse forms of knowledge by which various cultures know the world, the conviction that the sciences cannot be the only source of knowledge, and the doubt that science can always offer irreversible results. All of this has contributed to a greater balance in the relations

---

30. Cf. M. Schlick, *Tra realismo e neo-positivismo*, Bologna: il Muligno, 1983; R. Carnap, *Der logische aufbau der welte*, Hamburg: Felix Meiner Verlag, 1961.
31. Cf. K. Popper, *The Logic of Scientific Discovery*, London: Hutchinson, 1980.
32. Cf. T. Kuhn, *The Stucture of Scientific Revolutions*, University of Chicago, Chicago 1962.
33. Cf. I. Lakatos - A. Musgrave, *Criticism and the Growth of Knowledge*, Cambridge University Press, Cambridge 1970; I. Lakatos, *The methodology of scientific research programmes*, Cambridge University Press, Cambridge 1978; P.K. Feyerabend, *Against Method*, NBL 1975.
34. Cf. B.C. van Fraassen, *The Scientific Image*, Oxford University Press, Oxford 1980.

between studies of the natural sciences and humanistic studies, and therefore to a lessening of the apparent difficulties.

We should not neglect to emphasize the great importance of the decline of mechanistic thinking regarding the clarification of the nature of scientific knowledge and the relative importance of other forms of knowledge. In the twentieth century the abandonment of old mechanistic schemes was resisted by some scientists who had come to regard mechanism as more than just one interpretation but as *the* interpretation of the world. During this last century, however, the conviction has gradually emerged that neither mechanism nor any other understanding of the physical world should present itself as philosophy. To fall into this error is to seriously risk the integrity and development of the sciences themselves.

Werner Heisenberg wrote:

> The great discoveries related to individual natural phenomena are possible when we avoid determining in advance through generalizations of the essence of these phenomena.[35]

The dialectic that has worked itself out during these four centuries in the relationship between scientific knowledge and humanistic knowledge has brought an ever greater fragmentation of culture, whose various fields still tend to live independently as if in fixed compartments. It has been realized that such a fragmented culture leads to the denial of a truly human culture, since the unity of the person requires a coherent articulation of the "partial truths" coming from the various ways of knowing the single reality.

Overcoming this state of things in our contemporary culture is the great challenge to which university institutions are called today. Their task is to dedicate themselves to a true dialogue between humanistic and scientific fields of knowledge, understood as a pathway towards Truth. In doing so, they will be contributing to the overcoming of the difficulties of the past and to helping human consciousness move towards a unitary approach to knowledge.

---

35. W. Heisenberg, *Das Naturbild der heutigen Physik*, Hamburg: Rohwolt, 1955, p. 132.

# 3

# Chenu's Recovery of Theology as a Science

## Patricia Kelly

I N THIS CHAPTER, I shall show how the French Dominican Marie-Dominique Chenu (1895–1990), through his recovery of the medieval concept of theology as a science, proposes an alternative relationship between theology and science, one in which theology and science work together, to seek the truth of God's creation, which may be found in nature and through divine Revelation, the normal source for theology. Chenu suggested that the new appreciation of 'nature' in the twelfth century, which he linked directly to the rediscovery of Greek learning in the West from the ninth century onwards, influenced theology to the extent that it gradually became *sacra doctrina*, a science, rather than *sacra pagina*, the glossing or commentary on Scripture, which had dominated until this period.

### *'On whether Theology is a Science': STIa.1 ad.2*

In his article on 'religion and science' for the online *Stanford Encyclopedia of Philosophy*, Alvin Plantinga posits that in the contemporary context, "the most salient question is whether the relation between religion and science is characterized by *conflict* or *concord*."[1] Yet, for much of the development of what the West now thinks of as 'science,' such a relationship would simply not have been a question: from the ancient Greeks, through the Islamic scholars of the early medieval period, and up to the rise of modernity itself, holding a religious belief was not considered

---

1. Plantinga, Alvin, "Religion and Science," in Edward N. Zalta (ed.), *The Stanford Encyclopedia of Philosophy* (Summer 2010 Edition), <http://plato.stanford. edu/archives/sum2010/entries/religion-science/> accessed 1 August 2013. Author's emphasis.

incompatible with exploring the boundaries of knowledge and understanding, perhaps because holding a religious belief of some kind was itself normative. Indeed, as Plantinga points out, many of those we regard as "the early pioneers and heroes of modern Western science—Copernicus, Galileo, Kepler, Newton, Boyle, and so on" were Christians, indeed, 'serious' Christians.[2] It is only with the rise of Modernity, and the (French and British) Enlightenment(s)[3] that there has been an ever-increasing perception that 'Religion' and 'Science' should be separated. But eight centuries ago, when scholars in the West were rediscovering Aristotle, no such separation existed: both religion and science were part of what constituted knowledge.[4]

Thomas Aquinas (1225–74) begins his *Summa Theologiae* by asking a question which is pertinent to the present chapter: "[O]n what sort of teaching Christian theology is and what it covers" (*ST 1a.1*).[5] "Christian theology does not look like science [for it] advances from the articles of faith and these are not self-evident [principles]" (*ST 1a.1 ad.2*). By 'self-evident principles' are meant measurable and observable data: the movement of the stars, types of rock, the growth of trees. But, he answers, theology is indeed a science, for it develops from divine Revelation (see *ST 1a.1 ad. 2, ad. 3, ad. 4*); albeit a science which "is more theoretical than practical, since it is mainly concerned with the divine things which are" (*ST 1a.1 ad.4*).

Not only is theology a science; importantly, Aquinas clarified that it is the noblest of sciences, for theology "takes its principles directly from God through revelation, not from the other sciences" (*ST 1a.1 ad.5*); other sciences are "subsidiary and ancillary" (*ST 1a.1 ad.5*). Of course, this largely because the study of theology focuses "on God as principal and on creatures in relation to him, who is their origin and end" (*ST 1a.1 ad.3*); indeed, "in Sacred Science all things are treated of under the aspect of

---

2. Plantinga, 'Religion and Science.'
3. It is worth noting that, although French and British Enlightenment thinkers sought to separate religious faith from philosophical and scientific discourse, the German *Aufkläring* recognized no such distinction.
4. Latin *scientia*, from which the English term 'science' derives; it should be noted that English has lost the sense, retained in French *science* and German *Wissenschaft*, of 'science' as the pursuit of knowledge, which will lead to truth.
5. All citations from the *Summa theologiae* are taken from vol. 1, trans. Thomas Gilby OP (Cambridge: Cambridge University Press, 2006).

God: either because they are God Himself, or because they refer to God as their beginning and end" (*ST 1a.1. ad7*). For Thomas, revelation offers an explanation for and understanding of God, while *scientia* offers an account of the world; the *Scientia Sacra* thus offers an account of God, the unintelligible Being to whom human existence is directed, using reason. In this way the scientific method is applied to faith, resulting in theology, faith seeking understanding, becoming a science.

### Chenu the Medievalist

Chenu was at the forefront of what has become known as *ressourcement* theology,[6] perhaps the most significant development in twentieth-century Catholic theology, which provided crucial foundations for the work of Vatican II.[7] *Ressourcement* theology was marked by both the return to the sources of Christian doctrine—biblical, liturgical, patristic, medieval—with an additional attentiveness to their context and place within theology; and by an engagement with the world beyond the Church. In both these developments, the work of Chenu, as a historical theologian, and as a *théologien engagé*, was of crucial importance. Trained at the Angelicum, Chenu completed his doctoral thesis on "Contemplation in Aquinas," supervised by the twentieth-century *doyen* of Thomism, Réginald Garrigou-Lagrange, OP (1877–1964).[8] In 1920, he returned to Le Saulchoir, the Dominican novitiate then located in Belgium, where he was immediately recruited to the *Institut historique des études thomistes*, whose Secretary he became. The research group's focus was "to read and understand Thomas in his time... making him intelligible

---

6. On *ressourcement* theology, see Gabriel Flynn & Paul D. Murray (eds), *Ressourcement: A Movement for Change in twentieth-century Catholicism* (Oxford: OUP, 2012); Denys Turner (Guest Ed.), *IJST* 7/4 (2005); Hans Boersma, *Nouvelle théologie and Sacramental Ontology* (Oxford: OUP, 2010); Jürgen Mettepenningen, *Nouvelle Théologie New Theology* (London: Continuum, 2010).

7. Flynn describes the *ressourcement* theologians as 'the harbingers of the new era of openness, ecumenism, and dialogue inaugurated at the Second Vatican Council' (Flynn, 'Introduction' in Flynn & Murray, *Ressourcement*, 1–19 (9).

8. Garrigou-Lagrange dominated Aquinas studies at the Angelicum during the twentieth century. Chenu remembered him as not only a 'generous' supervisor, but also 'a master of spirituality,' who had indeed 'restored in Rome the great tradition of teaching spiritual theology,' an expert on John of the Cross, and whose lectures were attended by 'crowds of young students.' (Jacques Duquesne, *"Un théologien en liberté:" Jacques Duquesne interroge le Père Chenu* (Paris: Éditions du Centurion, 1975) 38) (All translations from foreign language sources are my own).

for today;"[9] the founding of the *Institut* meant that "the application of the historical method to the study of St Thomas thus became one of the characteristics of Le Saulchoir."[10] The centre was strongly influenced by the Dominican historian, Pierre Mandonnet,[11] who retired from Fribourg to Le Saulchoir; the first chapter of his *St Dominique l'idée, l'homme et l'œuvre*, "Christianity at the dawn of the thirteenth century," is the perfect metaphor for its aims, to research Thomas Aquinas and "the Middle Ages as the cultural locus in which he lived."[12]

Chenu's earliest articles focus on Thomas, some exclusively, some in the light of his interaction with both his Dominican contemporaries—notably the English Dominican Richard Kilwardby (1215–79)[13]—and their twelfth-century predecessors, particularly Alain of Lille,[14] the Chartres School,[15] and the twelfth-century Victorines.[16] Chenu was adamant that there had been "a three-stage Renaissance of Antiquity of which the Italian Quattrocento was simply the completion:"[17] without

9. Duquesne, *Chenu* 49.
10. M.-D. Chenu, *Une École de Théologie: Le Saulchoir* ed Giuseppe Alberigo *et al.* (Paris: Cerf, 1985), 113.
11. Pierre Mandonnet OP (1858–1936) held the Chair of Ecclesiastical History at the Dominican faculty of Fribourg from 1891 until 1918, authoring influential works on major medieval figures and their contexts including *St Dominique: l'idée, l'homme et l'œuvre* (posthumously published in 1938); *Siger de Brabant et l'Averroisme latin au XIIIeme siècle* (1899); and *Dante le théologien* (1935). He was also the founder of the *Bibliothèque thomiste*, a monograph series dedicated to the study of Thomas and his precursors.
12. Duquesne, *Chenu* 49.
13. Kilwardby (*c.* 1215–79), who taught at both Paris and Oxford, was a contemporary of Thomas and an early commentator on Aristotelian logic. 'In his day, he was famous for his knowledge of Augustine's works, and shows an equally assiduous reading of Aristotle's' (Chenu, *La Théologie comme Science au XIIe siècle*, 3rd edn (1969), p. 50).
14. Alain of Lille (d. 1202) was a prolific twelfth-century theologian and poet-philosopher. Probably a teacher in the Paris schools who retired to Montpellier and died at Cîteaux, his works include the *Ars catholicae fidei, Ars Praedicandi, De Fide Catholicae: contra Haereticos, Valdenses, Iudaeous et Paganos, Regulae Theologicae,* and the philosophical poems *De planctu naturae* and *Anticlaudianus.*
15. The School of Chartres was one of the many cathedral 'schools,' whose heyday was in the mid-twelfth century (*c.* 1125–1180) with notable scholars such as Bernard of Chartres, Thierry of Chartres, and Gilbert de la Porrée.
16. The School of St Victor was, Abelard recounts, founded by his former teacher, William of Champeaux at the monastery to which he retired. The most famous scholars of this late-tenth/early-eleventh-century monastic school are Hugh of St Victor and Richard of St Victor.
17. Chenu, 'Nature and Man. The Renaissance of the Twelfth Century,' in *Nature Man, and Society in the Twelfth Century* MART 37 (Toronto: University of Toronto Press, 1997) 1–48 (1).

the Carolingian and Ottonian Renaissances during the ninth and tenth centuries, on which the twelfth-century Renaissance built, the fifteenth-century Renaissance simply could not have happened, for the scientific knowledge which underpinned it would not have been present in the West.

Two early publications[18] demonstrate that already, "the problem of the unity and immutability of the faith"[19] was at the heart of Chenu's historical theology. These articles are "given over to the distinction which Thomas introduced between the object of faith considered as such, and its expression by the believer, who is conditioned by his own cultural context."[20] Alberigo further notes that "the years that followed [the publication of these articles] were full of research on medieval theology, which would be brought together in *La théologie comme science au XIIIe siècle* in 1927,[21] *La Théologie au XIIe siècle* in 1957, and the wonderful *Introduction à l'étude de saint Thomas d'Aquin* in 1950."[22] Jolivet observes that, "while hardly 25 pages between them, [these articles] are full of meaning and promise,"[23] adding that from this point onwards there was "not a single year" in which Chenu did not publish on the medieval period. Chenu, he surmises, "never stopped being a medievalist, but practical urgencies imposed their own demands."[24]

These 'practical urgencies' informed what has been described as Chenu's 'incarnational theology,'[25] the integration

---

18. 'Contribution à l'histoire du traité de la foi. Commentaire historique de la IIa-IIae, q.1, a.2,' *Mélanges thomistes* 3 (Paris: Vrin, 1923), 123–40 repr. in *La Parole de Dieu I. La foi dans l'intelligence* (Paris: Cerf, 1964), 31–50; 'La raison psychologique du développement du dogme' *RSPT* 13 (1924), 44–51; repr. in *La Parole de Dieu I*, 51–8. 'Contribution' discusses not only Thomas' discussion of the question (II.IIae.1.2: 'Whether the object of faith is something complex by way of a proposition') but also examines how the question was dealt with by his immediate predecessors.
19. Chenu, 'Contribution' p. 34.
20. Giuseppe Alberigo, 'Christianisme en tant que l'histoire et "théologie confessante",' in Alberigo *et al.*, *Le Saulchoir*, 11–34 (20).
21. This was initially a lengthy article, re-published as a small book in 1943, and a 3rd edition in 1957. All citations are from the 3rd printing of the 3rd edition (1969).
22. Alberigo, 'Christianisme,' 20.
23. Jolivet, 'Les études,' 70–1.
24. Jolivet, 'Les études,' 71.
25. Claude Geffré, 'Le réalisme de l'incarnation dans la théologie du Père M.-D. Chenu,' *RSPT* 69/3 (1985) 389–99; Christopher Potworowski, *Contemplation and Incarnation. The Theology of Marie-Dominique Chenu* (Montreal: McGill-Queen's University Press, 2001).

of theology into the world—the urgent need for the evangelization of workers, for instance—guided by his insistence that "the theologian works on a history... their data is events, the response to an *economy*."[26] He could not, says Le Goff, "conceive of a theology, nor of a history of theology, working outside of the history of the societies in which this theology acted and expressed itself,"[27] whether in biblical studies, late antiquity, the middle ages, or modernity. Precisely part of his critique of the then dominant neo-Thomist school of theology was that it removed theology from the context—real life—in which its practitioners were living. Theology, he insisted, should not only relate to real life, but also derive from faith; a theology "constructed outside of the experience of faith [was] a still-born theology."[28]

Chenu's bibliography is overwhelmingly weighted towards the medieval period. Jolivet,[29] basing himself on Duval's 1967 bibliography of some 355 titles, published in *Mélanges*,[30] suggests around 70 specifically medieval works; Potworowski's 2001 bibliography (which includes translations, re-editions, and even a handful of posthumous publications) lists 1396 titles, approximately half of which are medieval in theme.[31] Yet Chenu's achievement was to demonstrate precisely that medieval theology was not an arcane series of disputes in some long-distant past, but a serious engagement with a fast-changing world, which was of great relevance to, and instructive for, twentieth-century theology. The urgency for theologians was, he insisted from the earliest days of his career, "to be present to our days, just as Thomas Aquinas and Bonaventure were to theirs."[32] Aquinas and the Schoolmen thus became, for Chenu, examples

---

26. Chenu, 'Position de la théologie,' *RSPT* 24 (1935), 232–57; repr. in *Parole I*, 115–38 (129).
27. Jacques Le Goff, 'Le Père Chenu et la société médiévale,' *RSPT* 81/3 (1997), 371–80 (371).
28. Chenu, 'Position,' 118.
29. Jolivet, 'Les études,' 70ff.
30. André Duval, 'Bibliographie du P. Marie-Dominique Chenu (1921–1965),' in Duval (ed.), *Mélanges offertes à M.-D. Chenu*, Bib. Th. 37 (Paris: Vrin, 1967), 9–29.
31. A sample, of the 391 titles published between 1921 and 1945 reveals that, in addition to the 18 'Bulletins' for the *RSPT*, Chenu published 199 titles which directly deal with medieval theology.
32. Chenu, *Le Saulchoir*, 123–4.

for modern theologians to follow, demonstrating how theologians were to be engaged (*engagés*) in the contemporary world.

## Chenu's retrieval of theology as a science

As a historical theologian, Chenu was always careful to locate theology within its intellectual context, as, for instance, in his 1950 monograph, *Introduction à l'étude de Saint Thomas d'Aquin*. The greatest influence on the development of scholasticism, and in turn, the thought of Aquinas, was not, he argued, Aristotle, nor the twelfth-century Renaissance, but rather, the 'evangelical Renaissance' which took place between the mid-twelfth and early-fourteenth centuries: the search for the 'apostolic life;'[33] the growth of groups such as the Humiliati and the Poor Catholics, and indeed, the mendicant orders such as the Dominicans,[34] who sought to live apostolic poverty in common; and the rise of preaching and popular teaching in the vernacular.[35] This "return to the sources"[36] was, he noted, inspired by "the perennial problems of nature and grace," one which bore fruit in "a new Christian awareness of nature and of man,"[37] as exemplified, in the thirteenth century, by the theological work of Thomas himself. In this final section, it is shown that, for Chenu, the development of theology as a science required *both* the use of 'scientific tools,' *and* a profound appreciation of the original 'data of faith.' Theology, in other words, may only properly flourish by applying the scientific method to faith, in order to achieve its understanding.

---

33. The high medieval period was marked by lay Catholic groups inspired by the Gospel to live simply and preach the Good News. Waldensians, Humiliati, and Poor Catholics were all condemned for public preaching (then reserved to bishops), and in some cases heresy, but the Humiliati and Poor Catholics were reconciled by 1210. The Cathars, in southern France were notoriously put down for heresy during the late thirteenth century.

34. The Dominican Order, was founded to combat the Cathar heresy then dominating the region between Toulouse and Barcelona. Dominic 'adopted the apostolic life, modelled on Luke 10, as the most promising way of combating the heretical "evangelical" preachers' (Simon Tugwell OP (ed), *Early Dominicans* (Mahwah NJ: Paulist, 1982), 16); the Order sought to preach the Gospel, lead a simple life, and earn their food and shelter by begging (hence 'Mendicant'). Approved by Honorius III by 1217, Dominicans were present in five Provinces by the time of Dominic's death in 1221, including at the University of Paris.

35. Chenu, *Introduction*, 38ff.

36. Chenu, *Introduction*, 41.

37. 'Monks, Canons, and Laymen in search of the Apostolic Life,' in *Nature and Man*, 202–38 (203).

As described above, Chenu acknowledged that there were indeed three 'Renaissances:' the Carolingian/Ottonian Renaissance of the ninth/tenth centuries; the twelfth-century Renaissance; and the fifteenth-century Renaissance, or Quattrocento. As he pointed out, theology relies on the pedagogical tools to hand in contemporary culture; and so the "Carolingian 'Renaissance,' the twelfth- and thirteenth-century 'Renaissance,' and the fourteenth-century 'Renaissance' were all key factors in its evolution in the West."[38] By Carolingian Renaissance, Chenu meant the reform of education which took place under Charlemagne: his establishment of schools across the Holy Roman Empire; his attracting to his court many of the great minds of the period, such as Alcuin of York (*c.* 740–804);[39] and the development of the 'seven liberal arts,'[40] which "made up the programme for theology at that time," of which "grammar, or the science of words, was the most important, and the most used."[41] Already in the ninth century, the study of the *sacra pagina* was influenced by the recovery of the classical arts of grammar and dialectic (logic), as demonstrated by the monastery of Corbie (Picardy), famous for the scholars Ratramnus († *c.* 870) and Radbertus Paschasius († *c.* 860), and their dispute about the use of the term 'corpus mysticum:'[42] did it refer to the Eucharist (the sacramental body of Christ), the Church (the 'mystical body' of Christ), or to the historical body of Jesus of Nazareth, the Christ? The tenth-century pope, Sylvester II, also famous as the mathematician Gerbert of Aurillac,[43] wrote his own treatise on

---

38. *La Théologie Comme Science*, 16.
39. Alcuin a Northumbrian monk, was educated at York, and recruited by Charlemagne to join his court, probably by 770. Charlemagne placed Alcuin in charge of the palace school at Aachen, where he introduced the liberal arts, and produced a number of teaching manuals on them, before returning to monasticism as Abbot of St Martin at Tours. He is widely regarded as one of the intellectual leaders of the Carolingian Renaissance.
40. The *trivium*, grammar, dialectic (logic), and rhetoric provided the foundations from which the *quadrivium*, arithmetic, geometry, astronomy, and music could be taught.
41. Chenu, *La Théologie Comme Science*, 18.
42. See Henri de Lubac, *Corpus Mysticum. The Eucharist and the Church in the Middle Ages* trans. G. Simmonds, R. Price, C. Stephes; ed. L.P. Hemming and S.F. Parsons (London: SCM Press, 2006) 28ff.
43. Gerbert (*c.* 946–1003; pope 999–1003) was known in his day as a mathematician and scientist, who had effectively re-introduced the study of the *quadrivium* into the monastic schools in France. There is some speculation that he learned these skills during his time as a young man travelling in Arabic Spain, where (as in Sicily) Islamic scholars were rediscovering and developing

the Eucharist, while the eleventh-century scholar, Berengarius of Tours, returned to the Corbie dispute, using dialectical tools to argue about the material presence of Christ in the Eucharist and the importance of the words of consecration. The question of how Christ was present in the Eucharist, and how and when this presence became 'real,' depended on the use of the arts of the *trivium*, rediscovered in the ninth-century Carolingian schools.

Chenu argued that, from the early-twelfth century onwards, the arts of the *trivium* and *quadrivium* merged with the theological study of the Scriptures to begin a development into a mature theology, informed by scientific tools, which would become scholasticism. His focus on the twelfth-century pre-scholastic theologians, such as the Chartres and St Victor schools and Alan of Lille, enabled him to chart the crucial shift in medieval theology from *sacra pagina* to *sacra doctrina*, theology as a science. Alan's own *Regulae theologicae*—"the method according to which faith-knowledge, like any other intellectual discipline, was organized and built upon internal principles which gave it a scientific turn and value"[44]—was based upon the scientific methodologies he and his contemporaries studied. As demonstrated above, this move took place precisely thanks to "the discovery of Aristotle and the assimilation of Greek reason by Christian theology" in the West.[45] But this assimilation was not without its problems: the application of the liberal arts to theology during the twelfth and thirteenth centuries was strongly contested.

Perhaps inevitably, the fact that theology had been 'tainted' by possible heresy as had happened during the Eucharistic disputes of the ninth and eleventh centuries, meant that the overt use of scientific tools such as logic and grammar in theology was highly suspect. By the early-thirteenth century, there was concern at the university of Paris about "the intrusion of philosophy"[46] into the study of theology; of particular concern to Pope Gregory IX (pope 1227–41), in his 1228 letter to the faculty, was the entry of Aristotle—pagan philosophy, recovered through Islamic science—into the bounds of theology. Gregory

---

Ancient Greek scientific knowledge.

44. Chenu, 'Nature & Man,' 48.
45. *La Théologie comme Science*, 101.
46. *La Théologie comme Science*, 31.

was fighting a losing cause however, as by the late-thirteenth century "Aristotle's epistemology had been boldly settled in the sacred territory of revelation."[47] But it was no coincidence, Chenu asserted, that this establishment of Aristotelian science as a tool for theology came about at precisely the same moment as the religious recovery of evangelicalism, one of whose fruits was the founding of the Dominican order itself. He argued that from the mid-eleventh century, theology had been less concerned with the grammatical and dialectical disputes exemplified by the discussions about the Eucharist, and more concerned with the meaning of faith and revelation; questions of God and salvation; a recovery of the importance of the Scriptures; and a new spirituality which focused on the *vita apostolica*.

Yet this new focus on revelation was not entirely independent of Greek learning. The twelfth century, suggested Chenu, "featured an essentially religious discovery of the universe through the discovery of Nature."[48] It was the rediscovery of Aristotle during this period which "revealed nature and humanity to thirteenth-century minds;"[49] indeed, Chenu drew an analogy between the twelfth-century recovery (in the West) of Greek works, and what he describes as the 'discovery' of nature, evident in the work of "the naturalistic artists who [now] sculpted little scenes of animal or human life on the capitals of cathedrals;"[50] "rational proofs in courts of law instead of the mystical expedient of trials by ordeal;"[51] and theologians themselves, whose work on the Greek classics had, more often than not, led to a changing world view—one which perceived "the universe as an entity... a cardinal point among the Ancients, [which] was now revived."[52]

The recovery of ancient understandings of the workings of the universe led to disputes among scholars even within Schools: "[t]he creation narrative in Genesis was interpreted as recounting the natural play of the elements... God was not absent, but it is the very laws of nature that reveal his presence

---

47. *La Théologie comme Science*, 101.
48. 'Nature & Man,' 48.
49. *Théologie comme Science au 13eS*, 22.
50. 'Nature & Man,' 10.
51. Nature & Man, 5.
52. Nature & Man, 5.

and his action."[53] The praise of and search for understanding of nature was perceived as praise for God, the divine creator, and as an attempt to understand him: the wonder of "life's ordered energies, its instincts, its laws, and its freedoms, the rhythmic movement of the seasons...,"[54] as described for instance in the *De Planctu Naturae*, composed at the very end of the twelfth century by the great pre-Scholastic Alan of Lille, was in itself a way of pondering the wonder of God.

The twelfth century was also, Chenu noted, "a turning point in medieval civilization; so marked was the transformation that took place in the material conditions of life that it has been possible to speak of a 'technological revolution.'"[55] His understanding of this 'turning point' was wide-ranging: Le Goff suggests that he was "the first one to emphasise that the movement towards the towns and the movement towards universities, in other words, scholasticism as a whole, went hand in hand,"[56] and indeed Chenu several times noted the 'significant choice' of "setting up a priory in the middle of a city,"[57] adding that, "the 'university' of studies, within which these schools grouped themselves spontaneously, is one of the institutions of the new city."[58] Crucially, and ironically, the rediscovery of nature led to its control by knowledge, whether of the laws governing the universe, or of the technology which might better subdue it. For Chenu, this was summarized by the "two extremes that the twelfth century brought together" — humanity as "simultaneously an image of the world ... and an image of God."[59]

## Conclusions

Chenu was an outstanding theologian, for whom theology was no intellectual exercise confined to the ivory tower, but rather, a discipline which grew from the search of faith for understanding, and which had an obligation to be "present to our

---

53. Nature & Man, 16.
54. 'Nature & Man' 18.
55. Nature & Man, 39.
56. Jacques Le Goff, 'L'intellectualité dominicaine au moyen âge et sa relation au monde de la ville et de l'université' in Duval (ed.), *Moyen-âge et modernité* 57–65 (57).
57. Chenu, *Aquinas and his role*, 15.
58. *Aquinas and his* role, 16.
59. 'Nature & Man,' 33.

world." At the same time, he was also a respected medieval historian, and he drew on this to inform his theology. Just as the theologians of the eleventh and twelfth centuries had reflected theologically on social changes such as the growth of towns and cities, international trade, and technological changes, so it was incumbent on twentieth-century theologians to engage with the economic and social changes which had arisen out of industrialization and globalization. As a theologian of work, and as a pastor, he was deeply involved in the Church's missions to industrialized sectors of society, particularly with the Christian Worker movements and the Worker Priests.

Chenu's recovery of medieval theology proposes two further areas in which contemporary theologians may learn from the medieval Masters. First, the controversy around integrating Aristotle into scholastic theology was about both 'pagan' philosophy, and, of more contemporary import, about the contribution knowledge mediated through Islamic scholarship can make to Christian theology. In an age when Christian-Muslim dialogue is of ever-increasing importance, it is useful for theologians and scientists to remember just how much *scientia* we owe to Islamic scholars from the ninth century onwards. Second, Chenu's recovery of theology as a science in the thirteenth century provides theologians and scientists with a model for theology and science to work better together to understand the world.

## 4

# A "COSMIC AUTHORITY PROBLEM"
# Lawrence Krauss and Thomas Nagel's
# Approach to the Question of God

### Brendan Purcell

To GET THE FLAVOR of English-speaking popular science writing, here's how Stephen Hawking and Leonard Mlodinow begin their *The Grand Design*: they ask, "What is the nature of reality? Where did all this come from? Did the universe need a creator?" And further on: "Traditionally these are questions for philosophy, but philosophy is dead. Philosophy has not kept up with modern developments in science, particularly physics. Scientists have become the bearers of the torch for discovery in our quest for knowledge."[1] Lawrence Krauss, a theoretical physicist, recently published *A Universe from Nothing: Why there is Something Rather than Nothing* (New York: Atria Paperback, 2013) where he gives an extremely useful survey of some of the latest theories in physics. My problems won't be with that, but with Krauss's philosophical or anti-philosophical presuppositions. Having discussed some of these presuppositions, I'll move on to Thomas Nagel's *Mind and Cosmos: Why the Materialist Neo-Darwinian Conception of Nature is Almost Certainly Wrong* (New York: Oxford University Press, 2012), a rather more critical approach to a different area of scientific endeavour.

### I

**1. Scientistic methodology:** I'll begin with Krauss's methodological presupposition, that only questions asked within the

---

1. Stephen Hawking and Leonard Mlodinow, *The Grand Design* (London: Bantam Press, 2010), pg. 5.

context of the natural sciences are genuinely rational ones. He writes, for example that "Whenever one asks 'Why?' in science, one actually means 'How?' 'Why?' is not really a sensible question in science because it usually implies purpose..." (xiv) So for him, "The important question...becomes not *'Why?'* but *'How* does our solar system have nine planets?' (xv) which he repeats later, consistently eliding the question about existence: "I am going to assume what this question really means is to ask, 'How is there something rather than nothing?' 'How' questions are really the only ones we can provide definitive answers to by studying nature." [144]

He excuses himself for taking:

> a rather flippant attitude toward this concern, because I don't think it adds anything to the productive discussion, which is, "What questions are actually answerable by probing the universe?" I have discounted this philosophical issue, not because I think those people who occupy themselves with certain aspects of it are not trying hard to define logical questions. Rather, I discount this aspect of philosophy here because I think it bypasses the really interesting and answerable physical questions associated with the origin and evolution of our universe. No doubt some will view this as my own limitation, and maybe it is. But it is within that context that people should read this book. I don't make any claims to answer any questions that science cannot answer... (xvii)

In fact he does claim to deal with questions that "science cannot answer." For Krauss, the question, "Why is there something rather than nothing?" while it "is usually framed as a philosophical or religious question... is first and foremost a question about the natural world, and so the appropriate place to try and resolve it, first and foremost, is with science." (xxiii)

He complains about "those who choose to ignore empirical data...who...require the existence of something for which there is no observable evidence whatsoever (like divine intelligence) to reconcile their view of creation with their a priori prejudices..." (118) However, as a scientist, Krauss too is bound by the requirement of evidence, and he hasn't provided any that would prove that in every conceivable issue, the only adequate evidence is what he calls "observable evidence" — that provided by the methods of say astrophysics. As philosopher Eric Voegelin writes:

> the popular assumption that mathematical natural science is the model of science par excellence, and that an operation not using its methods cannot be characterized as scientific, is neither a proposition of mathematical science, nor of any science whatsoever, but merely an ideological dogma thriving in the sphere of scientism.[2]

To bolster his position that the only rational inquiry possible is that made by natural scientific investigation, Krauss asks his readers to jettison their non-scientific judgments and values — unsurprisingly there's no reference to the relevant philosophical area of metaphysics:

> ...it is *extremely significant* that a universe from nothing... that arises naturally, and even inevitably, is increasingly consistent with everything we have learned about the world. This learning has not come from philosophical or theological musings about morality or other speculations about the human condition. It is instead based on the remarkable and exciting developments in empirical cosmology and the particle physics that I have described. (142–43)

He concedes that "It certainly seems sensible to imagine that a priori, matter cannot spontaneously arise from empty space, so that *something*, in this sense, cannot arise from *nothing*. But when we allow for the dynamics of gravity and quantum mechanics, we find that this commonsense notion is no longer true. That is the *beauty* of science, and it should not be threatening. Science simply forces us to revise what is sensible to accommodate the universe, rather than vice versa." (151)

**2. Forgetfulness of the subject:** The paperback edition of *A Universe From Nothing* concludes with a "Q & A with the author" where he repeats that "Our common sense should derive from the universe, rather than vice versa." (205) He continues: "There are questions we can address effectively via empirical

---

2.  Voegelin, *Anamnesis: On the Theory of History and Politics* (Columbia, MO: University of Missouri Press, 2002), 376. Voegelin is using the term introduced by von Hayek, 'scientism'—also used in this essay—as indicating the radically non-scientific assertion of philosophical claims as if grounded in observations of natural science.

methods and questions we can ask that don't lead to physical insights and predictions. The trick is to tell the difference between the two."

If only Krauss had spent some time reflecting on his own conscious data of questioning—say what he's done in his book, by putting together an exciting run-through of recent developments in theoretical physics including a judicious use of diagrams and illustrations. Such reflection would have yielded greater awareness of the complementarity of and difference between image and insight. It would also have shown the difference between a hypothesis and a judgment—where the judgment goes beyond insight by weighing the evidence for the insight, leading to its being verified or falsified.

In these correlated activities he'd have been able to get an insight into himself as a knowing subject, certainly 'deriving' images from the surrounding universe, but necessarily going beyond the data presented to grasping its meaning and judging whether that insight is correct or not. If he couldn't be persuaded to take up Bernard Lonergan's *Insight: A Study of Human Understanding*, he could do worse than acquaint himself with Michael Polanyi's *Personal Knowledge*. Krauss doesn't advert to the fact that the questions of natural science only occur because there are questioners, and questioning, by its very nature, goes beyond material presentations to formulate a very non-material idea, concept, hypothesis, theory, which further needs to be transcended by a judgment of their truth. As he says, "Most theories are in fact wrong." (208)

**3. Multiverses shaved by Ockham's Razor:** Perhaps because of his lack of an articulation of the process of scientific knowledge, in his endorsement of multiverses and his affirmation of previous but utterly unknowable states of our own universe, Krauss seems happy to cut himself adrift from scientific evidence altogether. So he accepts "the possibility of other 'universes'—regions that have always been and always will be causally disconnected from ours, like islands separated from any communication with one another by an ocean of space..." (126) Again: "The possibility that our universe is one of a large, even possibly infinite set of distinct and causally separated universes, in each of which any number of fundamental aspects of physical reality may be different, opens up a vast new possibility for understanding our existence." (175) "Causally separated universes" would mean universes with no observable impact on our own.

Not only does Krauss affirm synchronic non-connectedness, he seems to support diachronic non-connectedness too. He proposes what seems to be a version of the Steady State theory, where each recurrence wipes out the memory of the previous state. He envisages a rapidly expanding universe getting flatter and flatter, "even as the energy contained within empty space grows as the universe grows. This phenomenon happens without the need for any hocus pocus or miraculous intervention... when the energy in empty space gets turned into an energy of real particles and radiation, creating effectively the traceable beginning of our present Big Bang expansion. I say the traceable beginning because inflation effectively erases any memory of the state of the universe before it began." (150)

What about Ockham's (or Occam) razor here? How can there be any scientific consideration of something for which there's no possibility of evidence or verification either across space or time? Isn't this a stranger leap than theists' arguments for God? He himself writes: "Occam's razor suggests that, if some event is physically plausible, we don't need recourse to more extraordinary claims for its being." (146) Unsurprisingly for such scientistic statements, Krauss has a scientistic reason for making them:

> Nevertheless, a multiverse, either in the form of a landscape of universes existing in a host of extra dimensions or in the form of a possibly infinitely replicating set of universes in a three-dimensional space as in the case of eternal inflation, changes the playing field when we think about the creation of our own universe and the conditions that may be required for them to happen. (176)

**4. Krauss on 'God':** But to understand what lies at the heart of Krauss's book, I suggest we take a look at his notion of God as creator and at what he means by 'nothing.' Firstly, his rather anorexic notion of God, as at best an earlier inhabitant of the series of events comprising the universe:

> ...the declaration of a First Cause still leaves open the ques-
> tion, "Who created the creator?" After all, what is the dif-
> ference between arguing in favor of an eternally existing
> creator versus an eternally existing universe without one? ...
> this metaphor of an infinite regression may actually be closer
> to the real process by which the universe came to be than a
> single creator would explain. (xxii)

In his *The God Delusion*, Richard Dawkins assumes as
Thomas Nagel puts it, that God is "a complex physical inhabitant of the natural world." But, as atheist philosopher Nagel
points out, no one—perhaps other than Dawkins and we can
add, Krauss—considers God to be some kind of intramun-
dane phenomenon, subject to a question of the type asked by
Dawkins, "who made God?" Rather, Nagel continues: "If the
God hypothesis makes sense at all, it offers a different kind
of explanation from those of physical science... The point of
the hypothesis is to claim that not all explanation is physical,
and that there is a mental, purposive, or intentional explanation more fundamental than the basic laws of physics, because
it explains even them."[3] It's hardly surprising Krauss's notion of
God is so thin, given his amazing reading of Aristotle, and his
misreading of the classical Thomist articulation of why God's
existence is necessary:

> The apparent logical necessity of First Cause is a real issue
> for any universe that has a beginning. Therefore, on the ba-
> sis of logic alone one cannot rule out such a deistic view of
> nature....Consider, in the light of our modern picture of cos-
> mology, for example, Aristotle's suggestion that there are no
> First Causes, or rather, that causes indeed go backward (and
> forward) infinitely far in all directions. There is no begin-
> ning, no creation, no end. (173)

For starters, Aquinas ruled out the possibility of a rational proof for the world's having a beginning—he reckoned
this truth was only available to him as a believer.[4] As Norman
Kretzmann notes in his discussion of this matter in the *Summa
Contra Gentiles*:

---

3.  Thomas Nagel, 'The Fear of Religion,' *New Republic*, 23 October 2006, pg. 26.
4.  There's a brief discussion of this well-known view of Aquinas in my *From Big
    Bang to Big Mystery: Human Origins in the Light of Creation and Evolution* (Hyde
    Park, NY: New City Press, 2012), pp. 139–43.

He has thus already suggested in *SCG* that the *essential* relation of the created world to the omnipotent, beginningless creator is that of total existential dependence, not that of having been brought into existence for the first time, even if the created world was in fact brought into existence for the first time a finite number of years ago.[5]

And while Aristotle's God isn't the God of Jewish or Christian revelation, he certainly never made the statements Krauss attributed to him, which are easily contradicted in his *Metaphysics* or his *Physics*.[6]

Krauss acknowledges that Galileo, Newton, "and a host of other scientists over the years," have accepted that the universe, including ourselves, was "created by a divine intelligence." There is an interesting tentativeness to his philosophical and decidedly non-scientific judgment on the "two different conclusions" — theistic and atheistic — that can be made regarding the universe: "the final arbiter of this question will not come from hope, desire, revelation, or pure thought. It will come, if it ever does, from the exploration of nature." (142) Why could not a complementary physical and metaphysical inquiry include a question about nature's existence?

**5. Krauss on 'nothing':** Krauss chastises theologians for the "vague and ill-defined sense" in which they speak of 'nothing,' and of "the intellectual bankruptcy of much of theology and some of modern philosophy." For him, 'nothing' is every bit as physical as 'something,' especially if it is to be defined as the "absence of something." He describes 'nothing' "as the absence of space and time itself." (xxiv) Like an experienced poker player trying to distract his opponents, Krauss seems to throw cards on the table which look as if now you see his 'nothing' and now you don't:

---

5.  Norman Kretzmann, *The Metaphysics of Creation: Aquinas' Natural Theology in* Summa Contra Gentiles II, (New York: Oxford University Press, 1999), 150.
6.  Aristotle, *Metaphysics*, tr W.D.Ross (Oxford: Oxford University Press, 1966): "God is thought to be among the causes of all things and to be a first principle..." 983a8; "But evidently there is a first principle, and the causes of things are neither an infinite series nor infinitely various in kind... But of series which are infinite... and of the infinite in general, all the parts down to that now present are alike intermediates; so that if there is no first there is no cause at all." 994a1, 994a17f.

> In one sense it is both remarkable and exciting to find ourselves in a universe dominated by nothing. The structures we see, like stars and galaxies, were all created by quantum fluctuations from nothing. (105)

He speaks of "theoretical speculations based on considerations of a universe that could have arisen naturally from nothing, or at the very least, from *almost nothing.*" (148—Krauss's emphasis) A few pages later, he admits that "it would be disingenuous to suggest that empty space endowed with energy, which drives inflation, is really *nothing*... This is just the first step, however. As we expand our understanding, we will next see that inflation can represent simply the tip of a cosmic iceberg of nothingness." (152) Later he will write that "'nothing' means empty but preexisting space combined with fixed and well-known laws of physics. Now the requirement of space has been removed. But, remarkably, as we shall next discuss, even the laws of physics may not be necessary." (170) This leads to the final stage of Krauss's argument.

**6. No causation because 'chance' underlies everything:** As with Hoyle, Bondi and Gold's 1948 Steady State theory—which one might suspect was concocted because of the threat the Big Bang theory posed to their comfortable atheism—multiverses seem to have more to do with moving the goalposts regarding the question of creation than with any scientific evidence. Krauss goes on: "In the first place, the question of what determined the laws of nature that allowed our universe to form and evolve now becomes less significant. If the laws of nature are themselves stochastic and random, then there is no prescribed 'cause' for our universe." (176) He even admits that "there may be no fundamental theory at all." (177) Paul O'Hara, a professor of mathematics at Northeastern Illinois University, with a keen interest in theoretical physics, comments on this:

> Any serious mathematician would define this stochastic set of laws that he claims exists. The fact is he cannot do so because he has no idea what they are. Moreover, even if a stochastic set of laws did exist, it would simply mean that we have a coincidental aggregate of laws which have been ordered according to some type of indexing set. A coincidental set of laws are precisely that: a set of laws. The inevitable

question then arises as to where these sets of laws come from? Indeed, we cannot even classify them as laws unless there is some intelligibility that allows us to identify them as laws, as something from which we derive meaning.[7]

Faced with a mounting challenge to her position, Jocasta in Sophocles' Oedipus Rex invokes the goddess of blind fate: "Why should man fear since Chance (Tyche, in Latin, the goddess Fortuna) is all in all for him, and he can clearly foreknow nothing?" Maybe Krauss is channelling Jocasta a little here, with his over-reliance on chance as an explanatory factor. The problem is that the laws of probability employed for understanding particle physics wouldn't be 'laws' if they were 'random'—rather they have their own rationality as a meaningful grasp of for example the particle field recently verified with the discovery of the so-called 'God-particle.' Krauss seems so keen on denying any rationality to the notion of a divine creator that he will endorse multiverses—states of the universe on principle inaccessible to observation—and finally a notion of physical law so random it couldn't be caused by anything since it's intrinsically meaningless. Jocasta would have sympathised.

**7. Leibniz's question, "Why is there something rather than nothing?" resists Krauss's eclipsing**: Try as he might to eclipse that question, Krauss seems haunted by an origin of existence he has left unexplained. It's as if he's aware that despite his best efforts he hasn't even succeeded in satisfying himself:

> A simple answer is of course that neither empty space or the more fundamental nothingness from which empty space may have arisen, preexisted and is eternal. However, to be fair, this does beg the possible question, which might of course

---

7. Personal communication, July 1, 2013. Professor O'Hara goes on: "There is also another irony (in my opinion) in his pseudo-definition of claiming the existence of a set of laws that have no prescribed cause. It forms the basis of Russell's paradox. For if such a set existed, presumably one could then define the set of ALL those subsets of laws that have no cause, let us call it S. The question then is whether S has a cause or not. Whatever answer one gives will lead to a mathematical contradiction. For if S has no cause then it constitutes a set of subsets of laws that have no cause that has been caused by the application of a law of selection. While if S has a cause then it is the cause of the set of all uncaused laws. In other words Krauss has no grounds in mathematical logic for making his statements. It is a meaningless and irrational statement of someone pretending to use scientific method to deny scientific method. Such arguments have been long rejected in mathematics as stemming from ill posed definitions."

not be answerable, of what, if anything, fixed the rules that governed such creation. (174)

Krauss's closing remark, rather than at last taking up the argument, is a simple statement of scientific theory, that the universe had a beginning and will have an end—which leaves his core, Leibnizian question, utterly untouched: "In this case, the answer to the question, 'Why is there something rather than nothing?' will then simply be: 'There won't be for long.'" (180) And in the "Q & A With the Author" section at the end, presumably reflecting questions he's been asked on the lecture circuit, Krauss speaks with the same mixture of certainty regarding any philosophical inquiry and uncertainty regarding the natural scientific inquiry:

> Now, the state of no stuff may not be 'nothing' in a classical sense, but it is a remarkable transformation nevertheless. So the first form of 'nothing' is just empty space... And the remarkable non-miraculous miracle is that combining quantum mechanics with gravity allows stuff to arise from no-stuff. I then describe how it is possible that space and time themselves could have arisen from no space and time, which is certainly closer to absolute nothing. Needless to say, one can nevertheless question whether there is nothing, because the transmission is mediated by some physical laws. Where do they come from? That is a good question, and one of the more modern answers is that even the laws themselves may be random, coming into existence along with universes that may arise. This may still beg the question of what allows any of this to be possible...(206)

**8. Ideologists' prohibition of questions:** The political philosopher, Eric Voegelin wrote about the prohibition of radical questioning that can be found in the ideologies of the last few centuries, for example in Auguste Comte's remark that questions about origins and ends are "necessarily forbidden" to the positivist (for Comte, natural scientific) mind. Karl Marx has a similar prohibition of questions about existence in his 1844 *Economic and Philosophical Manuscripts*: "Do not think, do not question me."[8] And Krauss adds his own prohibition, bolstered

8.   See Eric Voegelin's discussion of Comte and Marx in his *Science, Politics, and Gnosticism*, in *Modernity Without Restraint, Collected Works of Eric Voegelin*, Vol. 5, ed. Manfred Henningsen (Columbia, MO: University of Missouri Press,

by his quoting Darwin as a chapter heading: *"It is mere rubbish, thinking at present of the origin of life; one might as well think of the origin of matter."* (75) Later, having said that the Leibniz question "may be no more significant or profound than asking why some flowers are red and some are blue. 'Something' may always come from nothing... what is really useful is not pondering this question..." (178) It's precisely through the ideological prohibition of questions that Krauss performs the eclipse of the entire reality of Judeo-Christian-Greco-Roman culture, offering in return that abstracted aspect of it that can be investigated by the natural sciences—without color, sound, taste, without truth, without moral goodness, without transcendence; above all, without argument.

Unfortunately, Professor Krauss's *A Universe from Nothing* is not an untypical example of what Heidegger called "the forgetfulness of being" in English-speaking intellectual culture. For a far more balanced treatment of how some issues arising in the natural sciences can only be dealt with by philosophy, we'll now turn to a recent publication of one of the most highly regarded philosophers of that culture, Thomas Nagel's recent *Mind and Cosmos*.

## II

**1. Scandalous introduction:** "The Heretic: Who is Thomas Nagel and why are so many of his fellow academics condemning him?"[9] was the title Andrew Ferguson, senior editor of *The Weekly Standard*, gave to his review of Nagel's *Mind and Cosmos: Why the Materialist Neo-Darwinian Conception of Nature is Almost Certainly False*, which appeared in September 2012. He opens with a hilarious description of an "interdisciplinary workshop" on "Moving Naturalism Forward" held in the Berkshires, Massachusetts, a month later than the publication of the book. It was attended by an array of leading materialists, including Richard Dawkins, Daniel Dennett, Jerry Coyne, Alex Rosenberg (author of *The Atheist's Guide to Reality*), James Ladyman and Don Ross (authors of *Everything Must Go: Metaphysics Naturalized*). Ferguson writes:

---

2000), pp. 262–65.
9.   In *The Weekly Standard*, March 25, 2013.

A video of the workshop shows Dennett complaining that a few—but only a few!—contemporary philosophers have stubbornly refused to incorporate the naturalistic conclusions of science into their philosophizing, continuing to play around with outmoded ideas like morality and sometimes even the soul. "I am just appalled to see how, in spite of what I think is the progress we've made in the last 25 years, there's this sort of retrograde gang," he said, dropping his hands on the table. "They're going back to old-fashioned armchair philosophy with relish and eagerness. It's sickening. And they lure in other people. And their work isn't worth anything—it's cute and it's clever and it's not worth a damn."

There was an air of amused exasperation. "Will you name names?" one of the participants prodded, joking. "No names!" Dennett said. The philosopher Alex Rosenberg, author of *The Atheist's Guide*, leaned forward, unamused. "And then there's some work that is neither cute nor clever," he said. "And it's by Tom Nagel." There it was! Tom Nagel, whose *Mind and Cosmos* was already causing a derangement among philosophers in England and America.

Dennett sighed at the mention of the name, more in sorrow than in anger. His disgust seemed to drain from him, replaced by resignation. He looked at the table. "Yes," said Dennett, "there is that." Around the table, with the Power-Point humming, they all seemed to heave a sad sigh—a deep, workshop sigh. Tom, oh Tom...How did we lose Tom...

Since Nagel is one of the best-known analytic philosophers, *Mind and Cosmos* has had an explosive impact, tearing into the manicured lawns of English-speaking intellectual culture. This is all the more surprising since it developed topics Nagel has been exploring all his philosophical life in books like *The View From Nowhere*, *The Last Word*, and celebrated essays like "What Is It Like To Be a Bat?" The echoes of the explosion could be heard in the unusually high-pitched tones of the many negative reviews it received, nicely encapsulated in Simon Blackburn's comment: "If there were a philosophical Vatican, the book would be a good candidate for going on to the Index [of prohibited books]."[10]

---

10. Simon Blackburn, 'Thomas Nagel: a philosopher who confesses to finding things bewildering.' New Statesman November 8, 2012. In ten separate blog articles, philosopher Edward Feser has excellently documented 'Nagel and

**2. A cosmic authority problem:** No one has drawn open the curtain on the reasons for the prevailing naturalism/reductionism/materialism in English-language scientific and philosophical circles more widely than Thomas Nagel in his *The Last Word*, where he writes of the fear of religion, a fear he himself experiences: "I don't want there to be a God; I don't want the universe to be like that." (130) Not only has he a "cosmic authority problem"—for Nagel it's an underlying cultural issue of our time:

> My guess is that this cosmic authority problem is not a rare condition and that it is responsible for much of the scientism and reductionism of our time. One of the tendencies it supports is the ludicrous overuse of evolutionary biology to explain everything about life, including everything about the human mind. (131)

**3. But no reductionist materialism:** However, despite his atheism, in *Mind and Cosmos* Nagel distances himself from what he calls 'the orthodox view' of "physical-chemical reductionism in biology." (5) That 'orthodox view' he sees as owing some of its passion "precisely to the fact that it is thought to liberate us from religion" (12) and "as a manifestation of an axiomatic commitment to reductive materialism." (49) While rejecting the materialist-determinist view, he honestly admits his own preference "for an immanent, natural explanation...congruent with my atheism." (95) Throughout the book he will argue against "the secular theoretical establishment and the contemporary enlightened culture which it dominates." (127) So his concluding words are that

> I have argued patiently against the prevailing form of naturalism, a reductive materialism that purports to capture life and mind through its neo-Darwinian extension...I find this view antecedently unbelievable—a heroic triumph of ideological theory over common sense... (128)

**4. Epistemological reason for modern scientific reductionism:** Nagel diagnoses a historical reason for contemporary naturalism, noting that the "modern mind-body problem arouse out of the scientific revolution of the seventeenth

---

his critics' from October 22 2012 to June 18 2013 (available on edwardfeser. blogspot.com).

century, as a direct result of the concept of objective physical reality that drove that revolution." (35) Galileo restricted scientific investigation to externally perceivable space-time reality, with the mind relegated to merely subjective experience. The "secondary qualities like color, sound, and smell were to be analyzed rationally, in terms of the power of physical things, acting on the senses, to produce those appearances in the minds of observers." (35–36) This ruled out consciousness as a serious object of inquiry, but apart from the lived contradiction that scientific inquiry is grounded in consciousness, the existence of consciousness "seems to imply that the physical description of the universe, in spite of its richness and explanatory power, is only part of the truth..." (35)

In fact, given the inability of 'psycho-physical reductionism' to explain consciousness, this methodological failure "makes the currently standard materialist form of naturalism untenable, even as an account of the physical world, simply because we are parts of that world." (43) Throughout the book, Nagel will be arguing—as the book's title declares—that "the materialist neo-Darwinian conception of nature is almost certainly false." And for Nagel, the particular reasons for this is that an exclusively materialist view of nature can't account for consciousness, human knowing, and human freedom, which we'll very briefly refer to here.

### 5. Nagel's principal arguments against reductionism:

(i) **Consciousness:** Nagel asks: "What kind of explanation of the development of these organisms, even one that includes evolutionary theory, could account for the appearance of organisms that are not only physically adapted to the environment but also conscious subjects?" (44) For him, "a purely physical explanation" by its very nature, has to leave out the fact of "subjective consciousness....even if the physical evolution of such organisms is in fact a causally necessary and sufficient condition for consciousness." (45) But, for Nagel, "something must be added to the physical conception of the natural order that allows us to explain how it can give rise to organisms that are more than physical. The resources of physical science are not adequate for this purpose, because those resources were developed to account for data of a completely different kind." (46)

However, rejecting "psycho-physical reductionism leaves us with a mystery of the most basic kind about the natural order—a mystery whose avoidance is one of the primary motives for reductionism... And if physical science, whatever it may have to say about the origin of life, leaves us necessarily in the dark about consciousness, that shows that it cannot provide the basic form of intelligibility for this world." (53)

Nagel puts forward a dual explanatory strategy, "an ahistorical constitutive account of how certain complex physical systems are also mental, and a historical account of how such systems arose in the universe from its beginning." (54) The historical account "will depend on the correct constitutive account' which will be 'either reductive or emergent." Rejecting as inadequate the reductionist account, Nagel's emergent account "will explain the mental character of complex organisms by principles specifically linking mental states and purposes to the complex physical functioning of these organisms—to their central nervous systems in particular—in the case of humans and creatures somewhat like them." (54–55) But since an emergent explanation of consciousness as something "completely new" remains "fundamentally inexplicable" (56) Nagel seems to opt for another type of explanation. (We'll examine his reasons for rejecting divine creation later.)

The explanation Nagel seems closest to endorsing is Tom Sorell's 'neutral monism' as an alternative to "dualist, materialist, and idealist" approaches to the emergence of life, and later, of consciousness (57). As 'monism,' this avoids the unacceptability of 'dualism,' which would affirm two separate realities in a human being, spiritual and material, along with the equal unacceptably of asserting either one of these aspects on their own—'idealism' or 'materialism.' As 'neutral' it somehow smooths over the difficulty Nagel and other analytic philosophers have, faced with the stubborn refusal of human self-consciousness to be explained materialistically and their own inability to accept the complex unity of matter and spirit endorsed by Aristotle and Aquinas among others.

So for Nagel,

> Considered just metaphysically, as an answer to the mind-body problem, monism holds that certain physical states

of the central nervous system are also necessarily states of consciousness—their physical description being only a partial description of them, from the outside, so to speak. Consciousness is in that case not, as in the emergent account, an *effect* of the brain processes that are its physical conditions; rather, these brain processes are *in themselves* more than physical... (57)

So Nagel will propose "in contrast to classical dualism...an integrated naturalistic explanation of a new kind." (68–69) As far as I know, for Aquinas, the sense consciousness of animals, and indeed our own sensation, in itself is material, so it's possible the kind of developed neurological research Nagel looks forward to may in fact provide us with a 'neutral monist' explanation of consciousness at that level. What about the more specifically human levels of consciousness Nagel turns to in the next two chapters on 'Cognition' and 'Value'?

**(ii) Reason:** This is the second reality Nagel regards as incapable of explanation by 'evolutionary reductionism' which, as he's been saying, cannot account for consciousness "because of its irreducibly subjective character." (71) However, when he considers that type of consciousness involved in human reason, it is "not merely the subjectivity of thought but its capacity to transcend subjectivity and to discover what is objectively the case that poses the problem." (72) By contrast, animals live "in the world of appearances, and the idea of a more objective reality has no meaning." (73) Whether deliberately or not, Nagel echoes Parmenides and Plato when he writes that our recognition of "the distinction between appearance and reality, and the existence of objective factual or practical truth...goes beyond what perception, appetite, and emotion tell us." He includes here our basic capacity to arrive at truth, our capacity for "language and the possibilities of interpersonal communication, justification," where "to acquire language is in part to acquire a system of concepts that enables us to understand reality." (73)

If our reason is merely an effect of evolutionary causation, it's no longer whatever we mean by reason, that is, our capacity to affirm what is true on the basis of our understanding of reality. Nagel writes: "It is not possible to think, 'Reliance on my reason, including my reliance on *this very judgment*, is reasonable because it is consistent with its having an evolutionary explanation.'" (80–81) This is because our reason "enables us to escape from the world of appearance presented by our prereflective innate dispositions, into the world of objective reality..." (82–83) Intrinsic to our reason is its

> freedom—the freedom that reflective consciousness gives us from the rule of innate perceptual and motivational dispositions together with conditioning....The appearance of reason and language in the course of biological history seems, from the point of view of available forms of explanation, something radically emergent—if, as I assume, it cannot be understood behavioristically. (84–85)

For Nagel, reason can be envisaged as "a part of the lengthy process of the universe gradually waking up and becoming aware of itself." (85) But he's very much aware of the difficulty of fitting its emergence into an evolutionary framework, since it involves "the development of consciousness into an instrument of transcendence that can grasp objective reality and objective value." (85) He has already considered three kinds of 'historical' (in the sense of how something came about) explanation: "it will be either causal (appealing only to law-governed efficient causation), or teleological, or intentional." (58)

Given his argument against what he calls causal or reductionist explanation, Nagel is prepared to consider "either a teleological or an intentional solution." (88) He sees the rejection of teleological explanation as due to the seventeenth-century scientific revolution because teleology argues that some natural laws "are temporally historical in their operation." (92) In contrast, Nagel suggests that a 'naturalistic teleology' could be an irreducible part of the natural order. He adds that—where the third, intentional, kind of explanation involves divine creation: "I am not confident that this Aristotelian idea of teleology without intention makes sense, but I do not see at the moment why it doesn't." We'll discuss this issue in our comments on divine creation below, but Nagel seems to be unnecessarily opposing intentionality and teleology, where an Aquinas's treatment of the intrinsic teleology of created reality, following its own created laws, was already developed as a philosophy of secondary causation (discussed below).

**(iii) Freedom:** In his fifth chapter, on 'value,' Nagel argues that "Real value—good and bad, right and wrong—is another of those things, like consciousness and cognition, that seem at first sight incompatible with evolutionary naturalism in its familiar materialist form." (97) He agrees with Sharon Street that

> moral realism is incompatible with a Darwinian account of the evolutionary influence on our faculties of moral and evaluative judgment. Street holds that a Darwinian account is strongly supported by contemporary science, so she concludes that moral realism is false. I follow the same inference in the opposite direction: since moral realism is true, a Darwinian account of the motives underlying moral judgment must be false, in spite of the scientific consensus in its favor. (105)

What constitutes human orientation towards value, for Nagel includes the values of "honesty and dishonesty, justice and injustice, loyalty and betrayal." (113) Motivation or reasons for action at this level "involves a conscious control of action that cannot be analyzed as physical causation with an epiphenomenal conscious accompaniment, and... includes some form of free will." (113) As a result, "It is not compatible with a Darwinian conception of how the sources of our motives are determined.... Human action... is explained not only by physiology, or by desires, but by judgments." (114)

But whence arises our orientation towards value? On the one hand Nagel says that "we are evidently the product of evolution, and ultimately of a cosmic process... eventually producing intelligent beings capable of value judgments." (105–06) He maintains that consciousness, human cognition and freedom are "part of what a general conception of the cosmos must explain,' part of a process 'of the universe gradually waking up...'" (106) At the same time, he refuses to accept the adequacy of a biological explanation of the human: "I conclude that something is missing from Darwinism, and from the standard biological conception of ourselves." (111)

To answer the question of where our freedom comes from, Nagel returns to the three kinds of historical explanation he's mentioned earlier, causal, teleological, and intentional—noting that he's already ruled out a causal or deterministic explanation.

To account for "the appearance and development of value, a teleological explanation comes to seem more eligible. This would mean that what explains the appearance of life is in part the fact that life is a necessary condition of the instantiation of value, and ultimately of its recognition." But he sets aside intentional explanation, "even though it, too, could meet this condition." (121)

Developing his understanding of freedom as requiring a teleological explanation, Nagel speaks of organisms which *have* a good, so that things can go well or badly for them, but "in some of those organisms there has appeared the additional capacity to aim consciously at their own good, and ultimately at what is good in itself...On a teleological account, the existence of value is not an accident, because that is part of the explanation of why there is such a thing as life.... In brief, value is not just an accidental side effect of life; rather, there is life because life is a necessary condition of value." (122–23) He continues:

> This is a revision of the Darwinian picture rather than an outright denial of it...But even though natural selection partly determines the details of the forms of life and consciousness that exist... the existence of the genetic material and the possible forms it makes available for selection have to be explained in some other way. The teleological hypothesis is that these things may be determined not merely by value-free chemistry and physics but also by something else, namely a cosmic predisposition to the formation of life, consciousness, and the value that is inseparable from them.
>
> In the present intellectual climate such a possibility is unlikely to be taken seriously, but I would repat my earlier observation that no viable account, even a purely speculative one, seems to be available of how a system as staggeringly functionally complex and information-rich as a self-reproducing cell, controlled by DNA, RNA, or some predecessor could have arisen by chemical evolution alone from a dead environment.
>
> Some form of natural teleology...would be an alternative to a miracle—either in the sense of a wildly improbably fluke or in the sense of a divine intervention in the natural order. (123–24)

**6. Nagel on divine causation—positives and negatives:**
Although the question of divine causation or creation doesn't
get a chapter to itself in *Mind and Cosmos*, the question of God
crops up throughout the book. Integral to what Nagel calls reductive materialism is its erection of the natural sciences as the
exclusive source of rationality in human existence. Nagel undermines that assumption by referring to its essential epistemological presupposition, when he points out that science "is
driven by the assumption that the world is intelligible.... Without the assumption of an intelligible underlying order, which
long antedates the scientific revolution, those discoveries [by
the modern natural sciences] could not have been made." (16)
Further, that "intelligibility of the world... as described by the
laws that science has uncovered, is itself part of the deepest explanation of why things are as they are..." (17)

Nagel, despite his frank admission of a "cosmic authority
problem," along with his own atheist stance, does not rule out
divine creation as irrational, provided that it doesn't 'intervene'
in the universe's own intrinsic workings:

> A theistic self-understanding, for those who find it compel-
> ling to see the world as the expression of divine intention,
> would leave intact our natural confidence in our cognitive
> faculties. But it would not be the kind of understanding that
> explains *how* things like us fit into the world. The kind of
> intelligibility that would still be missing is the intelligibility
> of the natural order itself—intelligibility from within. That
> kind of intelligibility may be compatible with some forms of
> theism—if God creates a self-contained natural order which
> he then leaves undisturbed. (26)

I'd suggest that Aquinas' development of the notion of
caused or created or secondary causation, where each creature is to be understood in terms of its own created meaning
would not be too far from what Nagel is looking for when he
says he could accept a "self-contained natural order." Of course
I would rather do without Nagel's Deistic addendum: "which
he then leaves undisturbed," since the one act of divine creation includes continuous conservation in existence of beings
which freely develop according to their own inner logic. Here's
Aquinas on this:

> Nor is it superfluous, even if God can by himself produce all natural effects, for them to be produced by certain natural causes. For this is not a result of the inadequacy of divine power, but of the immensity of his goodness, whereby he also willed to communicate his likeness to things, not only so that they might exist, but also that they might be causes for other things. Indeed all creatures generally attain the divine likeness in these two ways.... By this, in fact, the beauty of order in created things is evident. (*Summa Contra Gentiles*, III, 70)

However, Nagel rules out "direct theistic explanation of systematic features of the world that would seem otherwise to be brute facts—such as the creation of life from dead matter, or the birth of consciousness, or reason. Such interventionist hypotheses amount to a denial that there is a comprehensive natural order." (26) While he praises the Intelligent Design theorists for having the courage to take on what he calls the materialist Neo-Darwinian conception of nature (10), he seems fixated on what seems like their (or William Paley's) invocation of a "divine intervention" whenever a 'gap' of intelligibility occurs in our understanding of the world. But a Thomistic understanding of creation, as we've mentioned, doesn't include interventions in the natural world—certainly the up to now inexplicable emergence of life from non-living materials, or of what geneticist Sean Carroll calls "the big bang of animal consciousness" are material phenomena whose origins can be considered to lie within the material world.

But Nagel can hardly expect to exclude the Leibnizian question that seems to bother Krauss so much—as we've seen, this is a question that astronomy has made available in a new way to philosophy, since if the universe has a beginning in time, its beginning in existence requires a rational explanation. Or if, as Aristotle held, along with some contemporary physicists, the universe is eternal, its existence is still eternally contingent or dependent. So perhaps the natural sciences and metaphysics are more closely related than Nagel would have them be—not as one interfering with the other, but both complementing each other, with their different questions and methods. That what Nagel calls "the birth of reason," concretely occurring with the conception of each human being, might pose another boundary question analogous to the Big Bang is something I've discussed in detail elsewhere.[11] Nagel himself offers no argument for excluding such a complementary approach to these boundary questions, other than suggest a "completely different type of systematic account of nature, one that makes these neither brute facts that are beyond explanation nor the products of divine intervention." He finishes that comment with "[t]hat, at any rate, is my ungrounded intellectual preference." (26) In other words, and disappointingly, he is unwilling to argue his case any further.[12] I think however we can tackle his treatment of divine action as an intervention by asking what we do when we know something.

**7. Spiritual/material interaction in human knowing as an analogy for divine creation of the material universe:** As we've seen, Nagel rules out an understanding of human knowing and human freedom that's intrinsically conditioned by matter. He also rules out dualism as explaining them. Though he doesn't quite get to Aristotle's hylemorphic approach, he's not far off it either. Lonergan's *Insight* famously quotes *De Anima* on its title page: "The mind grasps the forms through images." In other words, Aristotle, as developed by Aquinas and later Lonergan and others, would have no problem with a multicausal (material and spiritual) treatment of human knowing and human freedom. The spiritual component isn't an intrusion or an intervention in the material aspect of human understanding. We're only too aware of struggling to get the right images or words for our insights—and can't clearly formulate our thoughts without them. In fact, it's the spiritual component that largely guides the material aspect in the first place—for example, my quest to understand Nagel's book *Mind and Cosmos* led me to read every page of the materially presented text and to carry those read words, however imperfectly, in my memory. Similarly with the

---

11. Both the mystery of each individual human existence and of humanity in general is discussed in the last chapter of my *From Big Bang to Big Mystery: Human Origins in the Light of Creation and Evolution* (Hyde Park, NY; Dublin: New City Press; Veritas, 2012).

12. I had a similar sense of something missing in his otherwise riproaring demolition of Richard Dawkins *The God Delusion*, where, having shown how Dawkins takes for granted the existence of life, Nagel doesn't go any further with that argument, and himself pose the Leibnizian question (see Thomas Nagel, 'The Fear of Religion,' *New Republic*, 23 October 2006).

raw materials of our free decisions, namely, the images and feelings we need to steer in the direction of choosing the good.

In light of this multicausal understanding of these core activities of human existence, can we not suggest, with Aquinas, a multicausal approach towards creation, one where the spiritual component is even less 'intrusive' or interventionist than is the spiritual activity of the human mind on its material components? As we've seen, Nagel seems prepared to accept theistic causation provided it isn't of the God of the gaps kind that both William Paley and the proponents of Intelligent Design seem to favor. But, Aquinas' understanding of creation, I'd suggest, is analogous to the approach we have been taking to human understanding and freedom as unities of spirit and matter. God is utterly separate from what he has created, but his spiritual reality can order material creation in a way not utterly unlike how our understanding and freedom order our imagination, feeling and action.

Divine creation, called primary causation, both causes the entire universe to exist and maintains it in an existence which includes the intrinsic teleology uncovered both by astrophysics and evolutionary biology. It's this one divine (and so, intelligent) act of creation that accounts for the underlying rationality Nagel accepts is the presupposition for scientific understanding of the universe.

The material and material-spiritual components of the universe which comprise the work of creation, have their own intrinsic causation, a caused causation, which has been called secondary causation. In that sense, what constitutes and maintains the universe in existence is multicausal, with divine creation as its external cause and the created laws at the physical, chemical, biological, botanical, zoological and human levels as the series of internal causes. Far from drawing on divine action to explain human understanding and freedom, Aquinas insists on understanding them on their own terms. Bernard Lonergan's *Grace and Freedom* and *Verbum: Word and Idea in Aquinas* explore Aquinas's treatment of human understanding and freedom in terms of their own intrinsic intelligibility at the level of caused (or secondary) causation.[13] For Aquinas, in no case

---

13. *Grace and Freedom: Operative Grace in the Thought of St. Thomas Aquinas* (Lon-

does the primary causation of divine creation and conservation 'disturb' or 'intervene' in the sense of determining what I think or I choose.

Let's return to Nagel:

> But even a theist who believes God is ultimately responsible for the appearance of conscious life could maintain that this happens as part of a natural order that is created by God, but that does not require further divine intervention. A theist not committed to dualism in the philosophy of mind could suppose that the natural possibility of conscious organisms resides already in the character of the elements out of which those organisms are composed, perhaps supplemented by laws of psychophysical emergence. To make the possibility of conscious life a consequence of the natural order created by God while ascribing its actuality to subsequent divine intervention would then seem an arbitrary complication. (95)

There are two issues here. Firstly, as we've earlier mentioned, Nagel seems to have a mistaken interpretation of divine action. For Aquinas, it doesn't occur in time, so the notion of "further divine intervention" doesn't arise. From our viewpoint, creation unfolds at the physical and chemical levels from, say, the Big Bang, nearly 14 billion years ago, with life making—as far as we know—its first appearance less than 4 billion years ago, complex animal life from around 550 million years ago, and human life from, at least according to current anthropology, about 160,000 years ago. From the divine perspective, creation is just one single act, including its continual conservation. In that act there are no 'gaps.' Any gaps there are, are in the natural sciences, including biology, and their as yet inability to explain a whole array of events, from the first emergence of life, to the gap between prokaryotic and eukaryotic cells, to the emergence of animal consciousness, never mind the first occurrence of human reason in us.[14]

---

don: Darton, Longman & Todd,1971); *Verbum: Word and Idea in Aquinas* (South Bend, IN: University of Notre Dame Press, 1967).

14. Eugene V. Koonin, 'The Biological Big Bang model for the major transitions in evolution,' *Biology Direct*, August 20, 2007, online, spells out the current gaps in biological explanation—not only in our understanding of the emergence of life, but between eukaryotes and prokaryotes, them and the major animal phyla, and right up the evolutionary tree.

Secondly, as we've also noted before, Nagel seems committed at all costs to both acknowledging the non-materiality of human knowing and willing, and at the same time to affirming their intrinsic relatedness to matter—which would raise no boundary questions the way the Big Bang does. This brief essay can't of course go into that major discussion—why a whole range of what could be called soft materialists, including David Chalmers, Owen Flanagan, Colin McGinn, John Searle and others—insist human consciousness is something unique and somehow non-material, while still not being non-material or spiritual. I can only suggest that is because accepting the views of those who first discovered mind (in Bruno Snell's phrase), from Xenophanes, Heraclitus, Parmenides, to Socrates, Plato and Aristotle, followed by Augustine, Aquinas and others, of the intrinsic immateriality of the human mind, they would necessarily be led to its immaterial source. So that Nagel's "cosmic authority problem" can distort not only inquiries at the boundaries of astronomy and biology, but also at the heart of anthropology. At the same time, unlike Krauss, Nagel has braved the elements in questioning some of the major and successful ideological myths of our time, those of the exclusive authority of the natural sciences and the adequacy of Neo-Darwinian biology to explain every aspect of human existence.

# 5

# Modern Physics, the Beginning, and Creation

## Stephen M. Barr

### Beginning and Creation

SOME RELIGIOUS PEOPLE LOOK upon the discovery of the Big Bang as a scientific proof that the universe was created by God. Some atheists, on the other hand, point to speculative physics theories in which the universe had no beginning as showing that no Creator is needed. Both of these views are wrong and for the same reason. Both mistakenly equate the idea that the universe was created with the idea that the universe had a beginning some finite time ago. Admittedly, the Book of Genesis itself links creation and beginning when it says, "In the Beginning, God created the heavens and the earth." But even though the two ideas are connected, they are not the same. No less a theologian than St. Thomas Aquinas understood this very well. He believed it possible to prove philosophically that the universe is created, but not possible to prove philosophically that the universe had a beginning rather than having existed for infinite time.

At first, this sounds strange. Isn't it obvious that if something was created, it must have been created a finite time ago? That's certainly true of things that are "created" by human beings. If an artist paints a picture, that picture can be dated to the time when the artist painted it. Because the picture was made, it had a beginning. But the Church tells us that God does not create in the same way that human beings "create;" the comparison between the two is merely an analogy, and in this case somewhat misleading. So let us use a different analogy. Imagine a piece of paper that has been illuminated by a lamp forever, i.e. for time stretching infinitely into the past. Even though the illumination of the paper has always had a cause—namely the lamp—the illumination of the paper had no beginning. In a similar way, the existence of the universe must have a cause—namely God—but that does not necessarily imply that the existence of the universe had a beginning.

Creation has to do with why something exists at all, not with how long it has existed. One may put it another way: there is a difference between the *beginning* of a thing and the *origin* of a thing. The beginning of the play *Hamlet* is a set of words in Act I, Scene 1, whereas the origin of the play *Hamlet* is the creative mind of William Shakespeare. Shakespeare is the origin of the play in the sense that he is the reason that there is a play at all; he is the cause of its existence as a work of art. Similarly, the beginning of the universe is merely the set of events that happened in its first moments (about 14 billion years ago, according to present calculations), whereas the origin of the universe is the mind of God. Just as it would be silly to answer the question of why there is a work of art called *Hamlet* by pointing to its opening words, it would be silly to answer the question of why there is a universe by pointing to its opening events. Indeed, the opening of a play or the opening of the universe really have nothing to do with the cause of their existence. One could imagine a play that has no beginning or end—for example, a play whose plot goes round in a circle—and it would still require an author. Likewise, one could imagine a universe without beginning or end, and it would still require a Creator.

Now, even though the creation of the universe does not in itself imply that it had a temporal beginning, and even though, according to St. Thomas, God could have created a universe that had no beginning had he willed, the Book of Genesis tells us that our world did in fact have a Beginning, and both the Fourth Lateran Council and the First Vatican Council spoke of God creating the universe "from the beginning of time."

### Creation and Time

This brings us to a key point that was first understood by St. Augustine sixteen hundred years ago and only rediscovered by modern physics in the twentieth century. This point is that *the beginning of the universe was also the beginning of time itself.* In antiquity, many pagans mocked the Jewish and Christian teaching that the universe had begun a finite time ago, and they asked Jews and Christians what their God had been doing for all that infinite stretch of time before he got around to making the world. St. Augustine had a profound answer. He started with the idea that time, being a feature of this changing world, is also something created. Therefore, if time is passing, something created—namely, time itself—already exists, and hence creation has already happened. Consequently, it makes no sense to speak about any time passing "before creation." Time itself, as a created thing, began with the beginning of created things. God was not waiting around for infinite time before he created the world, said St. Augustine, for there is no such thing as "a time before creation." As he put it in Book XI of his *Confessions*, "Why do they ask what God was doing 'then' [before creation]? There was no 'then' where there was no time."

Modern physics has reached the same conclusion by a parallel route. Whereas St. Augustine started with the insight that time is something created, modern physics starts with the insight that time is something physical. After Einstein's theory of General Relativity, it became clear that space and time, rather than being something over and above physical events and processes, actually form a physical "space-time manifold" or fabric that is acted upon by other physical entities and acts upon them in turn. Space-time can bend and flex and ripple; and these distortions of space-time carry energy and momentum, just as all physical things do. Indeed, space-time is just as physical as magnetic fields are, or as rocks and trees. It follows therefore, that if the physical universe had a beginning (say, at the Big Bang), then space-time, as features of the physical universe, also began at that point. Before the beginning of the universe, therefore, there was neither time nor space; so that it in fact makes no sense from the viewpoint of modern physics to even use the phrase "before the beginning of the universe." Modern physics has vindicated St. Augustine's profound insight.

It is hard, indeed impossible, for the human mind to imagine time having a beginning. We must therefore again resort to analogies. Let us return to the analogy of a play. The plot of a play has a timeline in which its events can be located. If the play is in book form, we can locate its events by the page and line in which they occur. But the timeline of a book or play only applies to events within that book or play. It makes no sense, for example, to ask where in the timeline of the play *Hamlet* — on which page — the wizard Gandalf fights the Balrog or Sherlock Holmes meets Dr. Watson. Nor can one ask what happens in *Hamlet* after Act 5, since the play has only five Acts, and its internal time or plot-time simply ceases at the last word that appears at the end of Act 5, scene 2. Admittedly, one can, in a certain sense, ask what happens before Act 1 of *Hamlet*, because characters in the play recall and refer to prior events — for example the murder of Hamlet's father by Claudius. But strictly speaking, the plot-time *of the play*, measured by page and line, begins with the first line and ends with the last.

In a similar way, in the standard Big Bang theory there is a point (call it $t = 0$) that is the beginning of all physical phenomena, including space and time. As one (mentally) goes back in time toward that "initial singularity," space shrinks faster and faster, until at $t = 0$ it shrinks to nothing. Space and time wink out — or, looking at time in the right direction, they wink *into* existence at that point. In the standard Big Bang theory there are two possible fates for the physical universe: either it will expand forever, growing ever emptier and colder, or it will reach a maximum size and starts to collapse toward what is called the "Big Crunch." (Presently, the evidence favors the former possibility.) If the universe were to end in a Big Crunch, it would mean that space and time wink out at that point, a finite time in the future. That would be "finis" to the universe, and time would stop.

To push the analogy further, we see that the internal time of a play does not even apply to the doings of the play's author. Shakespeare getting married in not an event in *Hamlet* and has no location in *Hamlet*-time. In fact, Shakespeare thinking of ideas for the plot, or inventing characters, or composing soliloquys for *Hamlet* are also not events within the play and have no location in *Hamlet*-time (though they are, of course, the reason why certain things happen when and as they do in the play). Shakespeare is outside of his play and outside of its time. In an analogous way, the traditional Catholic teaching is that the space and time of this universe simply do not apply to God himself, in his divine nature.

Suppose, for example, we think of two physical events *A* and *B* that happen in our universe. Event *A* may come before *B* in physical time, and may perhaps be the cause of *B*, or at least influence *B*. God wills that *A* happen and that *B* happen, and he wills that the *occurring of A* come before the *occurring of B* in space-time. But God's *willing of A* does not happen before his *willing of B*. God's willing is not a physical process and therefore (unlike *A* and *B*) is not an event in space-time. The *effects* of his willing (namely, the events *A* and *B* themselves) do have a location in space and time, but that is not the same thing.

God's causing of *A* and *B* is on a different level altogether than *A*'s causing of *B*. Once again, the analogy of the play makes this clear. One may ask: Did Polonius die because the character Hamlet stabbed him? Or did Polonius die because Shakespeare wrote the play that way? The correct answer, of course, is "both." Hamlet stabbing Polonius is the cause *within the play* of Polonius dying. But Shakespeare is the cause of the whole thing—of the existence of the play *Hamlet*, of all its characters, all its events, and all the relationships among the characters and events, including where they occur within the play and how they fit into the causal structure of its plot. In an analogous way, physical events in this universe have spatio-temporal and causal relationships to each other, but the whole universe and all its events and internal relationships only exist because God conceived of them and willed that they should exist and have these relationships to each other. This is the classical distinction between primary and secondary causality. The causes *within* nature are called "secondary causes," whereas God (the "primary cause") is the cause *of* nature.

This raises the question of whether the beginning of the universe, which may have been the "Big Bang," was a "natural event." There is no reason coming from physics to doubt that it was. To say that an event is natural, is to say that it happens in accordance with the laws of nature. It is true that in the classical Big Bang theory the point $t = 0$ is a singular point at which the laws of physics break down, because various physical quantities would be infinite at that point (such as the density of energy and the Riemannian curvature of space-time). But it is known that the classical Big Bang theory cannot be a good description of nature very close to $t = 0$, because quantum mechanical effects should be important there, and present theories are inadequate to describe quantum effects at such high densities and curvatures. It is expected by most physicists that when (and if) the correct theory of "quantum gravity" is known, and the methods needed to apply it to the beginning of the universe are mastered, the singularity at $t = 0$ will melt away, and the laws of physics will be seen to apply at the beginning of the universe just as they do at later times. Nor is this merely a matter of philosophical prejudice. Long experience has taught physicists that when infinite quantities appear in their theories it is always because they have made unrealistic "idealizations."

That the Big Bang was very likely a "natural event," in the sense of obeying the laws of physics, is not a theological problem. It is like saying that the first sentences of *Hamlet* obey the laws of English grammar just as do all the other sentences in the play. One would expect nothing else. It is only a problem if one falls into crude anthropomorphism and imagines creation to be a physical process, like God setting a lighted match to a fuse. But that is not the Christian conception of Creation. Creation is the act by which God gives reality to the universe, and makes it not merely a hypothetical or possible universe, but an actually existing universe. He does not supply energy, as a match does to an explosive, he supplies reality. God supplies this reality equally to every part of the universe—all events at all times and places—just as Shakespeare equally brought forth every word of the play *Hamlet*.

## Was the Big Bang the Beginning of Time?

Even though the universe being created and the universe having a beginning are two logically distinct ideas, it is a fact that some atheists are discomfited by the idea of a cosmic beginning. For, even though a Beginning does not logically imply creation, it somehow suggests it. This led many in the scientific world to be prejudiced against the Big Bang theory and probably discouraged research on it and delayed its acceptance, as has been admitted by more than one prominent scientist. The Big Bang theory came out of the work of the Russian mathematician Alexander Friedmann and the Belgian physicist (and

Catholic priest) George Lemaître in the 1920's. And clear evidence that galaxies are flying apart as from some vast primordial explosion was announced in 1929. Yet even as late as 1959 a survey showed that most American astronomers and physicists still believed the universe to be of infinite age. Nevertheless, evidence in favor of the Big Bang theory accumulated, and became so strong by the 1980's that it was accepted by virtually all scientists. That the Big Bang theory is correct, however, does not necessarily settle the question of whether the universe had a beginning. There remains the possibility that the explosion that occurred 14 billion years ago was only the beginning of a certain part of the universe or a certain phase in its history, rather than the beginning of the universe as a whole. In fact, over the years many scenarios and theories of this type have been proposed. I will briefly discuss three of them, the bouncing universe, the cyclic "ekpyrotic" universe, and "eternal inflation."

I mentioned that in the standard Big Bang theory, the universe has two possible fates; it may expand forever or it may reach a maximum size and collapse toward a Big Crunch. If it does the latter, one may imagine that instead of the universe winking out at the Big Crunch, as usually assumed, it "bounces" and begins to expand again. If this were to happen, the Big Crunch would be the Big Bang of a new cycle of the universe. One can further imagine that such cycles of expansion, contraction, bounce and new expansion have been going on forever and will continue forever in the future. This scenario was proposed by Einstein himself in 1930. Can it be true? Almost certainly not, for several reasons. In the first place, it was shown many decades ago by the theoretical physicist Richard C. Tolman that in such a bouncing universe the cycles grow longer and longer (because of the increase of entropy). This means that they were shorter and shorter the farther one looks back into the past, and in such a way that the total duration of all past cycles added together was finite. That is, even in the bouncing universe scenario the universe had a beginning. Second, the entropy of the universe increases with each cycle, and from the amount of entropy that exists in the present cycle one can conclude that the number of past cycles was finite. Third, it is highly doubtful that a collapsing universe would bounce rather than simply ending in a Crunch. And fourth, it was discovered in 1998 that the expansion of the universe is currently speeding up (the scientists who discovered this were awarded the Nobel Prize in physics for 2011), so that it is doubtful that the expansion will reverse and lead to a collapse at all.

An interesting attempt to revive the idea of a cyclic universe was made about ten years ago by Paul Steinhardt and Neil Turok. In their scenario (called the "ekpyrotic universe"), there are two parallel universes, each having three space dimensions, which move toward each other through a fourth space dimension, collide, bounce, move apart, reach a maximum separation and then move toward each other again, repeating the cycle endlessly. This idea evades several of the problems of the original bouncing universe scenario. In the first place, the three-dimensional space of each parallel universe is always expanding, and the oscillations of contraction and expansion occur only in the fourth space direction (which we cannot experience or directly observe). This allows the scenario to be consistent with the fact that the expansion of our three space dimensions is accelerating and may never reverse. Second, the fact that entropy always increases with time is counterbalanced by the fact that the volume of three-dimensional space is also always increasing. Thus the entropy may always be increasing, whereas the *density* of entropy (i.e. entropy per volume) can be the same in every cycle, and the cycles can all have the same duration. Clever as the ekpyrotic idea is, however, it has been subjected to strong criticism as creating more theoretical problems than it solves. And even if it turns out to be viable as a theory of our universe, there is a powerful theorem proved by the physicists Borde, Guth, and Vilenkin, which implies the oscillations of such an ekpyrotic universe cannot have been going on for infinite past time. There had to be a first cycle.

Another attempt to construct a realistic theory of a universe without a beginning uses the idea of "eternal inflation" developed by Andrei Linde. The idea is that the universe as a whole is perpetually undergoing an "exponential" expansion. (What this basically means is that there is a time scale $T$, such that whenever a time $T$ passes the universe doubles in size.) Such an exponential expansion is called "inflation." Within this perpetually inflating universe, however, bubbles are continually forming within which space expands in the much slower fashion that characterizes the part of the universe that we can see — i.e. the part of the universe within our "horizon." (We have a horizon since we can only see light that was emitted after the Big Bang, and such light cannot have travelled a distance greater than about 14 billion light-years.) In other words, we are inside one of these bubbles, and it is so vast that it extends far beyond our horizon. In this scenario, the Big Bang that happened 14 billion years ago was not the beginning of the whole universe, but merely the formation of our bubble.

It should be noted that the idea of inflation was not proposed whimsically or arbitrarily, but because it resolves certain very difficult theoretical puzzles in cosmology. Most cosmologists therefore believe that our part of the universe did undergo inflation at some point in the past. And it has been shown that in a wide class of theories, if some region of the universe starts to inflate, inflation tends to take over and lead to eternal inflation. However, almost all theorists agree that "eternal inflation," while it may be "eternal into the future," probably cannot be "eternal into the past." One reason for this conclusion is the theorem of Borde, Guth, and Vilenkin referred to previously.

It seems impossible that we shall ever be able to determine by direct observation whether the universe had a beginning. We cannot see what happened before the Big Bang (if there was a "before"), because the Big Bang would have effaced any evidence of it. And even if we could, how could we ever tell by observation whether the past is infinite, since any *particular* past event that we observe must have occurred a finite time ago? Nevertheless, as we have seen, there are very strong *theoretical* grounds for saying that that the universe most probably had a temporal beginning.

This is a remarkable vindication of religious ideas. The pagan philosophers of antiquity, including Plato and Aristotle, believed that the universe had always existed. The idea of a beginning of the universe and of time itself entered Western thought from biblical revelation and from the profound reflection upon it of theologians such as St. Augustine. Until the twentieth century, however, modern science pointed the other way. The idea of a beginning of time seemed to make no scientific sense, and there seemed to be definite evidence that matter, energy, space and time had always existed and always would. For example, physicists discovered the law of conservation of energy, which says that "energy can neither be created nor destroyed." In chemistry it was found by that the quantity of matter does not change in chemical reactions. In Newtonian physics, the time coordinate, like the space coordinates, extends from $-\infty$ to $+\infty$. By the beginning of the twentieth century, many scientists looked upon the idea of a beginning of the universe as a relic of outmoded religious or mythological conceptions of the world. One finds, for example, the Nobel Prize winning chemist Svante Arrhenius saying in 1911, "The opinion that something can come from nothing is at variance with the present-day state of science, according to which matter is immutable." And the eminent physicist Walter Nernst (also a Nobel laureate) confidently declared that "to deny the infinite duration of time would be to betray the very foundations of science." When science did begin to see (from Einstein's theory of General Relativity) how time and space could have a beginning, and astronomical observations began to suggest that this might be true, many atheists had a hard time accepting it. And yet, despite all the doubts and misgivings of scientists, it seems to be the case after all that the universe had a beginning.

Faced with this fact, some atheists now pin their hopes on the idea that physics will "explain" this beginning. They believe that if the beginning of the universe can be shown to be natural, then the need for a supernatural cause of the universe would be avoided. We have already seen the mistake involved in such thinking. The beginning of the universe unfolding in accordance with natural laws no more renders a Creator unnecessary than the opening passages of a book unfolding in accordance with the laws of grammar renders an author unnecessary. Nevertheless, scientific theories of the beginning of the universe are interesting in their own right, even if they cannot bear the weight that atheists want to place on them.

## Quantum Creation of Universes

The most promising approach to "explaining" the beginning of the universe physically is a speculative idea called "quantum creation of universes." This idea is based on an analogy with the unquestionably real effect called the quantum creation of particles. This effect sounds mysterious and profound (and perhaps it is), but it is a fact of everyday life, familiar to all of us. Every time you walk into a dark room and flip on the light switch, you cause a flood of particles to be "created," namely particles of light (called "photons"). Other kinds of particles, even the massy kind that make up what we think of as ordinary matter, such as electrons or protons, can be created, though they have to be created in conjunction with "anti-particles." For example, an electron can be created along with an anti-electron (called a "positron"), and a proton can be created along with an anti-proton. Such "pair creation" can happen in several ways. For example, in an intense electric field, an electron-positron pair can suddenly appear out of the "vacuum," by what is called a "quantum fluctuation" or "quantum tunneling." Pair creation is a well-understood effect, which has been observed countless times in the laboratory, and the probability of its happening in various circumstances can be calculated precisely using the mathematical machinery of "quantum field theory."

When an electron-positron pair is "created," it isn't produced out of nothing. The electron-positron pair has energy (including the $mc^2$ each particle has from its mass). Since energy is "conserved," that energy must have come from somewhere. For example, when pair creation occurs in an intense electric field, what happens is that some of the energy stored in the electric field is converted into the energy associated with the masses of the electron and positron. One starts with an electric field and ends up with an electron, a positron and a somewhat weaker electric field. This "creation" is really just a transition of matter and energy from one form to another.

In quantum field theory, particles are "excitations" (or, if you will, disturbances) of "fields." So, for example, there is an "electron field" that extends throughout all of space and time. When that field is disturbed, waves develop in it, just as when a pond is disturbed ripples are produced. Quantum mechanics says that waves and particles are two different ways of looking at the same thing. So producing ripples in the electron field is equivalent to producing electron particles (and anti-particles).

We can push the pond analogy further. A pond that is still and a pond that has ripples in it are the same physical system in different states of agitation. In the same way, a situation in which there are no electrons or positrons, and a situation where there is an electron-positron pair (or several electron-positron pairs) are really just different states of agitation of the same system, namely the electron field.

Actually, one should not think of the electron field in isolation. It is merely part of a greater system that encompasses many other kinds of fields, including electromagnetic fields, neutrino fields, gravitational fields, quark fields, and so on. When an intense electric field results in electron-positron pair creation, what is happening is that a disturbance of the electromagnetic field is causing a disturbance of the electron field. This is similar to the way that a disturbance of the air (a breeze) might produce a disturbance of the water in a pond (ripples). In other words, the greater system, encompassing all the different kinds of fields that interact with each other, is making a transition from one of its many possible states, to another.

In physics, one always considers some definite "system," which has various possible "states," and is governed by dynamical laws (which depend on the nature of the specific system) and by the overarching principles of quantum mechanics (which apply to all systems). The dynamical laws and the principles of quantum mechanics allow one to calculate the probabilities of the system making a transition from one of its states to another. The system might comprise only electrons, positrons, and electromagnetic fields (in which case the dynamical laws are called "quantum electrodynamics"). Or the system could be a simple pendulum, or a hydrogen atom, or the whole universe.

The idea of the quantum creation of universes pushes the mathematics of quantum theory to its logical limit—and maybe even beyond it. Here one contemplates not merely a pair of particles suddenly appearing "in empty space" by a quantum fluctuation or quantum tunneling, but an entire universe—along with its space—appearing in this way. By "universe," in this context, is not meant the "totality of things," but rather a space-time manifold in which there exist fields that interact with each other. Our universe, for example, has one time dimension and at least three space dimensions (there may be more), and many kinds of fields, including electron fields, neutrino fields, quark fields, electromagnetic fields, gravitational fields, and so on. There could be other universes of the same kind. The idea is that one can go (by a quantum fluctuation) from a situation in which there are no universes, to a situation in which there is one universe; or more generally, from a situation with some number of universes to a situation with a different number of universes.

Several apparent difficulties with this idea immediately present themselves. The first of these is that the transition from no universes to one universe would at first sight seem to violate the conservation of energy. Presumably zero universes have zero energy, whereas one universe has a lot of energy, due to all the matter that is contained in it. It turns out, however, that a "closed universe" (one whose space closes in on itself, the way a circle closes in on itself) has zero total energy: the positive energy of the matter is canceled out by the negative gravitational energy. Thus, changing the number of such universes does not violate energy conservation.

A second apparent difficulty has to do with time. In a conventional calculation using the principles of quantum physics, one considers a system making a transition from one "state" at an earlier time (e.g. an intense electric field) to a different "state" at a later time (e.g. a weaker electric field plus an electron-positron pair). However, if we talk about a transition from a "zero-universe state" to a "one-universe state," in what sense is the zero-universe state "earlier"? Indeed, *at what time* was there such a state? We have already seen that time (at least as physicists understand it) is a feature of a universe: if there is no universe, there is no time. If we look at a universe that was produced by a quantum fluctuation, we can talk about time *within* that universe, and even about the beginning of that time, but not about a time "before the universe."

We have to be careful in discussing such scenarios of falling into the verbal trap of saying that "first" there was nothing and "then" there was something. In fact, the same sloppy way of speaking is sometimes found in theological discussions of "creatio *ex nihilo.*" When the Church teaches that God created the universe *ex nihilo*, she is not saying that there was once a time when there was no created thing (a contradiction in terms, as St. Augustine pointed out). Rather, she is saying that there was no time when there was a created thing that preceded the universe and out of which the universe was made. In fact, the meaning of *ex nihilo* is deeper. It is saying not only was the universe not temporally *preceded* by anything, but also that its creation *presupposes* nothing other than the will of God.

If that is what creation *ex nihilo* means, do quantum creation scenarios yield a physical mechanism of "creatio ex nihilo," as some seem to believe? One can restate the question in this way: do quantum creation scenarios presuppose "nothing" in explaining the origin of the universe? They certainly talk about a "state" with no universes. But a state with no universes is not nothing; it is a definite something—a "state." And that state is just one among many states of a complex physical system. That system has states with different numbers of universes. And all of those states are related to each other by precise rules: the dynamical laws and the principles of quantum mechanics that govern the system.

An analogy may be of help here. There is a difference between my having a bank account with zero dollars in it, and my having no bank account at all. As far as my finances go, they may both be said to be "nothing" or "no money"; but there is a big difference. A bank account, even one with zero dollars in it, is something. It presupposes that there is a bank and that I have some contract with that bank. Those facts presuppose, in turn, that a monetary system and a legal system are in place. My bank account is thus a small subsystem of a much larger and more complex system that is governed by precise rules. My account has various "states"; a state with zero dollars, states with a positive numbers of dollars, and even states with negative numbers of dollars (if my account is overdrawn). Transitions are not made between those states willy nilly, but in ways governed by the rules of the bank. For example, if the balance is negative and goes below some threshold, a rule may prevent further withdrawals and transitions to states with more negative balances. A state with a positive balance may periodically make a transition to a state with a lower balance, due to service charges. Moreover, the rules may only allow transitions between states containing money of a certain type: dollars, say, rather than rubles, pesos, or Euros. Moreover, I can have several bank accounts with zero balances, perhaps an account in an American bank with zero dollars and an account in a Russian bank with zero rubles. They are different and distinguishable accounts, which obviously shows that each of them is something, rather than nothing.

In the same way, even to talk about a "state with zero universes" presupposes a great deal, as we have seen, namely a rule-governed system with many possible states. In any quantum creation scenario, the rules governing the system allow the "zero universe state" to make transitions to states with one or more universes, but only if those universes have precise characteristics, such as a certain number of space dimensions and certain kinds of fields—just as the rule of my bank may only allow my account to make transitions to states with dollars rather than rubles. I can imagine many different rule-governed systems. In system $A$, the rules may only allow states whose universes have three space dimensions, whereas in system $B$ the rules may only allow states with universe having ten space dimensions. The "zero-universe state" of system $A$ is not the same entity as the "zero-universe state" of system $B$: they are subject to different rules that give them different potentialities.

So system $A$ is one where three-dimensional universes come into and out of existence, and system $B$ is one where ten-dimensional universes come into and out of existence. At this point one may ask which, if either of these systems is *real* as opposed to hypothetical. Are there *actually* three-dimensional universes coming into and out of existence, so that the mathematical laws of system $A$ are governing real events? Are there *actually* ten-dimensional universes coming into and out of existence, so that the mathematical laws of system $B$ are governing real events? Maybe one or the other is true, or maybe neither, or maybe both. Suppose system $A$ is real, whereas system $B$ is merely hypothetical. What made system $A$ real, but not system $B$? *That* is the question of "creation" in the theological sense of the word: what confers *reality* on system $A$ but not system $B$? And *that* is a question that the mathematical rules of system $A$ and system $B$ cannot possibly answer.

In his 1988 bestseller *A Brief History of Time*, the physicist Stephen Hawking correctly noted that a theory of physics is "just a set of rules and equations," and then went on to ask, "What is it that breathes fire into the equations and makes a universe for them to describe? The usual approach of science of constructing a mathematical model cannot answer the question of why there should be a universe for the model to describe." Strangely enough, it seems that Hawking forgot this key insight by the time he co-authored the book *The Grand Design* in 2010. He now thinks that a mathematical model can answer the question of why there should be a universe for the model to describe. The absurdity of that, which was not lost on the younger Hawking, can be made clear by a simple analogy. A story may be a work of fiction or of history; it may describe actual events or not. A story may tell of Stephen Hawking being born in 1942 and going on to become an acclaimed physicist. Another story may tell of Stephen Hawking being born in 1842 and becoming Prime Minister of the United Kingdom. Can I determine just by studying the words of the two stories which one describes a real state of affairs? Do the mere *words* of either story have in themselves the power to make real the events they describe? Does the mere fact that the second story purports to tell of something (i.e. Hawking, the future Prime Minister) coming into being in 1842 mean that the thing described *actually* did come into being? Obviously not. And neither does a mathematical model purporting to describing a universe coming into being by a quantum fluctuation mean that any such thing actually happens.

In sum, the theoretical ideas by which physicists hope one day to describe the beginning of the universe, while being very interesting, and possibly correct, are not alternatives to the Creator in whom Jews and Christians believe. That Creator is not a physical mechanism or phenomenon. He is the giver of reality.

# 6

# Science Is Not Scientific

## David Walsh

THE TITLE IS INTENTIONALLY provocative. It takes aim at the unquestioned authority in our world and asks it to explain itself. Can science be scientifically justified? One can almost hear the howls of dismissal. Science is what justifies all other claims to knowledge. It itself requires none. How could we have the temerity to suggest that it demonstrate its validity? What could be more reliable than that which tests all reliability? The supremacy of science arises from the invincibility of its method. For most purposes that is enough. The success of science is demonstrated in the ever more comprehensive access to reality it provides. We simply know the universe around us in more compelling ways. Yet we cannot quite eliminate a flickering awareness of the partiality of its perspective. To comprehend science we must, first, be prepared to go beyond it since science is incapable of understanding itself. The breakthrough occurs, second, when we realize that science is a reaching up toward the mind of God. Our conclusion, third, is that science is itself a spiritual reality, a transcending of all that merely is. It is the love of God even when it does not know God.

### Science cannot know itself

Science is not all of knowledge. We know this most of all when we notice its inability to ground its own first principles.[1]

---

1. "The fact that every science as such, being the specific science it is, gains no access to its fundamental concepts and to what those concepts grasp, goes hand in hand with the fact that no science can assert something about itself with the help of its own scientific resources." Martin Heidegger, *Nietzsche II: The Eternal Recurrence of the Same* (ed. and trans.) David F. Krell (New York: Harper, 1987), 112.

They can only be assumed. No one can demonstrate that scientific method provides a true access to reality. Even the fact that it has yielded a probably true account is no more than the accumulation of evidence. The leap of judgment by which we assert that the evidence is sufficient is not itself something based on evidence. It is the point at which we stand outside of evidence to render judgment upon it, for evidence cannot compel this assent. We must freely reach it in our capacity to transcend what is merely given. All working scientists know this interplay of thought and the material on which it works. They know the pull of competing theories and approaches; they know that they already soar far above them. It is the romance of uncovering hitherto unknown vistas that draws them on, refusing to remain within the limits of the routinely known. In many respects they are less interested in knowledge than in the quest for it. It is wonder, Aristotle remarked, that is the great opening of the human mind upon reality.

We forget, in other words, what makes science possible. It is only occasionally that our somnolence is ruptured by the thought of the strangeness of science itself. We sense that we are at the heart of a mystery. How can science be possible? How is it that at one point in the universe there exist small creatures, human beings, capable of contemplating it all? We are a part of the cosmic vastness and yet we can think of it as if we were not. A thinking reed, as Pascal called us, is simultaneously permanent and impermanent. Not only is it a wonder that we arrive at insights and judgments that form the building blocks of scientific theory, but its possibility is something that utterly escapes us. We know that the process of discovery involves creative events beyond our control. All our investigations of the universe depend on those flashes of genius we cannot summon and must accept in gratitude. Where our thoughts come from we do not know. But when we think about thinking as such we seem incapable of plumbing its mystery. Even Aristotle who gave us the formulation "thought thinking itself" (*noêsis noêseôs noêsis*), (*Metaphysics*, 1047b34) could only lead us to the boundary of the mystery. Its veil could not be removed. We are left with the admission of unsurpassability proclaimed by Einstein two millennia later. "The most incomprehensible thing about the universe is that it is comprehensible."[2]

That demarcation of a limit, however, must not be taken as the final word on the matter. Science may carry on without examining what it can never fully investigate, but philosophers have a calling to probe it as far as thought will allow. In an age dominated by science and the forgetfulness of its foundations, that responsibility assumes even greater importance. The present reflection is offered as just such a modest pondering of the imponderable. As such it lays claim to no greater expertise or information but only fidelity to the question that the existence of science itself calls forth. Like Socrates we concede that we have no greater wisdom but, like him, we realize that that concession is already the beginning of wisdom. Admitting a boundary to thought is not quite the same as reaching a wall that blocks our path, for it is already the beginning of a glimpse beyond it. In knowing the limit we have begun to see it as limit, that is, as what does not just limit us. Even if we have not moved much beyond it, we have in a small way grasped that possibility. We have not remained silent about what cannot be said, but have said more than can be said.

We have seen further than science itself can see for we have glimpsed what remains invisible within its perspective. Too occupied with what it investigates science scarcely gives a thought to itself. It does not see how extraordinarily different it is from anything it examines. This is the blindspot of every observer who cannot include the self within the field of vision. Yet even this analogy is not quite accurate for we have just defeated it. We have noticed what cannot be seen or known. Science can ask about the condition of its own possibility and in this way is fundamentally different from every other reality that simply is. The mind is present by way of never being fully present. Its capacity to know things contains both itself and what it knows. Self-consciousness is its deepest reality. The incomprehensibility, that so struck Einstein, has begun to diminish slightly. We begin to see that science rests, not on a method that infallibly guarantees its success, but on the capacity to stand outside of

---

2. Albert Einstein, *Ideas and Opinions*, trans. Sonja Bargmann (New York: Bonanza, 1954), 292.

the whole including the self that performs the contemplation. No artificial intelligence (a contradiction in terms) could ever raise the question of its own capacity, as Einstein did. Comprehension, it turns out, includes marveling at itself even if that reflection yields up the confession of its incomprehensibility. We do not know how it is possible for us to know the universe, the process that science accomplishes every day, but we do intuit the mystery by which it occurs. Science is contained in the mystery of its possibility. It is not a sheer mystery but one that, in being contemplated, discloses its presence.

Prior to the method of empirical verification is the readiness to embrace it as method. Like the rule of law, following scientific method is not a rule. It is the possibility of a rule as such. This means that the validity of science does not derive from its method but from the openness that embraces a methodical approach to the analysis of reality. Whence does the openness originate? That is of course what is mysterious. We cannot get behind it, but we can say something about it. We know that it is something given to us, an invitation we willingly and readily take up. In responding to the call of reality we discover our own capacity to set everything aside, even our own biological needs, for the brief moment in which we put ourselves in the position of what is not ourselves. We know by setting ourselves aside for the sake of knowing the other. Scientific method is no more than the formalization of that generosity. We become nothing so that the reality we investigate may occupy the whole of our attention. Objectivity is possible because subjectivity can be overcome. We do not live in ourselves but in the whole universe. While occupying a particular place and time we disclose our capacity to embrace every place and time. Nothing lies beyond the reach of our minds. Nothing is so alien that it cannot be comprehended. The inwardness that reaches everything outside of us demonstrates that we are utterly different from all that we consider. It is that unlimited openness that makes it possible for us to follow the canons of scientific method without imposing any preconditions. Wanting nothing in return we can come to know reality as it is. We have transcended it. That is the perspective of science that can with difficulty be glimpsed from within its practice but never encountered in any reality other than the scientist.

## Science seeks the mind of God

Science can in other words understand everything except science itself. This is a revision of Einstein's observation, but one that calls attention to the great intellectual challenge science confronts today. For most of its modern development science could safely ignore itself as it explored the nature of the universe around it. But gradually as the scope of its mathematical penetration became ever more comprehensive it could not avoid pronouncing on the nature of the whole. The theory of everything that Einstein proposed as the goal of physics would have to include the genesis of reality itself. Stephen Hawking, for example, cannot resist pronouncing on the question of creation. His latest book attempts to establish the possibility that the universe may be one of many universes that are capable of coming spontaneously into existence.[3] God is rendered obsolete. Other scientists, notably Richard Dawkins and Daniel Dennett, undertake a more aggressive critique of the notion of God.[4] He has become an outdated delusion to be discarded by a scientific worldview that can now stand on its own feet. What is the value of a God hypothesis that can play no role within our comprehension of the world? One would almost be inclined to agree with them, except that their protest against God suggests that he cannot be so easily set aside. Even the atheists are curiously absorbed with him. They constantly recall what they wish to reject. Perhaps the whole imbroglio arises from a deeper unease that cannot quite be acknowledged. Could it be that the place of science itself cannot be assured without a mind that transcends it? If the physicist is no more than a thinking speck of matter perhaps what is thought is equally insignificant.

Dependence and rivalry with a divine creator seem inherent to the scientific enterprise. We are after all aiming to comprehend reality from a God-like point of view. But this presupposes that such a viewpoint is possible, for we cannot even approach it if it is not real. This is the great crisis that rumbles beneath the surface of contemporary science. Talk of a "God particle"

---

3. Stephen Hawking and Leonard Mlodinow, *The Grand Design* (New York: Bantam, 2010).
4. Richard Dawkins, *The God Delusion* (Boston: Houghton Mifflin, 2006); Daniel Dennett, *Darwin's Dangerous Idea: Evolution and the Meanings of Life* (New York: Simon and Schuster, 1996).

or of a theory that explains everything carry something of the bravado that dares not confront the most troubling implication. That is, that such a perspective would have to include itself or risk the incompleteness that would overturn it. If science is as contingent as everything it studies then its knowledge is also contingent. It is ephemeral. Probability may be the closest that science approaches in making its truth claims but it cannot afford to regard that assertion as itself merely probable. Somehow somewhere it must be anchored in the more than probable. Science is the absolute assertion of probability. Like the weather forecasts, the employment of percentages allows them to claim one hundred percent accuracy. The premise of probability is certainty. Statistics as a discipline is not statistically true. Ancient science did not suffer from the same impediment since it knew that it stood within the arc of the first principle or ground of all things, from which it sought to derive the order of the cosmos. Modern science with its shift to the empirically verifiable could long overlook its own derivation from a lingering absolute. It could discourse in probabilities without attending to the nature of that discourse itself. But now that it aims at a comprehensive worldview it cannot simply bypass itself. It has no choice but to provide its own grounds by displacing God in reaching for God-like comprehensiveness.

The curious character of an independence that underlines its dependence can now be understood. The spectacle of a science that seeks to eradicate God, and thereby proclaims his ineradicability, is puzzling until we understand its source. A science of contingency cannot itself be contingent. It must arise from a necessity that insists that, even though the universe is not necessary, science itself is. The cosmos can only be comprehended from the perspective of that which escapes its contingency. It is by accounting for the whole that the authority of science is established, for then it has comprehended the condition of its own possibility. By contrast, invocation of a Creator would constitute an affront to the unsurpassability of science. It would be to appeal to an extrinsic explanation for what can only be compelling if it arises from within the intrinsic realm. Needing nothing beyond itself, science can now enjoy the supremacy of that which exists in undiminished serenity. Ancient science understood that contemplation was participation in the life of the gods, while modern science has vaulted directly into that highest attainment of autarky. Science is no longer reading the mind of God; it has identified itself with the mind of God. Its ambition must outstrip its character as a science of contingency because it intuits its untenability as science on any other basis. Like Nietzsche, science has no choice but to become God because it knows that only God's knowledge is true.

The impossibility of the aspiration only becomes explicit when science turns its focus toward human origins. Then it becomes evident that human beings are reducible to the biochemical ingredients that constitute them. Their emergence is sufficiently accounted for in some version of Darwininian natural selection. Evolutionary emergence becomes the comprehensive theory of life, including human life. The shock wave that assaults religion is only the most notorious impact of the theory of evolution. Less noticed are the disturbances that ripple across the self-understanding of science. Darwin himself confessed to the unease that troubled him when he thought of the status of his own theory. Was it any more than the convictions a monkey might harbor, supposing there were convictions in a monkey brain?[5] It was clear that the prospect that his own science might be no more than the feverish working of a particular organism had unnerved him. He had begun to contemplate what has become a commonplace of neuroscience in our own day. That is, that thought, including the thought of neuroscientists themselves, is nothing more than electrochemical events within the brain. The difference is that we no longer even voice the hesitations that Darwin admitted. We are too awed by the prestige of science to point out any contradiction in its view of the universe, especially when the conflict involves its basic presuppositions. There cannot be anything in the universe that cannot be analyzed into its material constituents. Not even science itself can be permitted to stand in the way of science.

---

5. "With me, the horrid doubt always arises whether the convictions of man's mind, which has been developed from the mind of the lower animals, are of any value or at all trustworthy. Would anyone trust in the convictions of a monkey's mind, if there are any convictions in such a mind?" Charles Darwin in a letter to W. Graham, 1881. *The Life and Letters of Charles Darwin*, ed. Francis Darwin (New York: Basic, 1959), 285. See the discussion in Brendan Purcell, *From Big Bang to Big Mystery: Human Origins in the Light of Creation and Evolution* (Hyde Park, NY: New City Press, 2012).

Naturally the suppression of inconsistency must involve a range of defense mechanisms. The simplest is avoidance of the questions that might trouble it or, when they do occur, a flat rejection of their relevance or, in the last resort, denunciation of the questioners as deluded. The vehemence with which any murmuring against the monopoly of materialistic explanations is greeted confirms the discomfort. As a consequence it takes a brave soul to publicly critique the regnant naturalistic worldview. Scientists themselves can only do so by strictly separating their spiritual convictions from what is scientifically authorized. No right thinking person could dispute the regnant materialist paradigm although, occasionally, a gadfly will suggest that it is badly in need of an overhaul.[6] The scorn heaped on such a suggestion is proof of its status as unquestioned orthodoxy. Allegiance is socially enforced rather than reached through mutual agreement. We are in the curious situation where science itself, in the sense of the rigid requirements of professional conformity, is the principal obstacle to the openness of inquiry. One is simply prohibited from pursuing certain lines of questioning. Scientism is in danger of supplanting science. Defensiveness may have arisen from the clashes between science and religion that have periodically erupted, but resistance to the possibility of a paradigm shift is surely the point at which science moves furthest away from science. This is the big insight of Thomas Kuhn's famous book on *The Structure of Scientific Revolutions*. He narrates the history of science as a series of disjunctive leaps that establish a new stabilization. At each of those decisive turning points it is the validity of science itself that is at stake as it struggles to choose between loyalty to the dominant paradigm or the intellectual expansion required to build a new one.

It is hardly too dramatic to say that we are at just such a juncture today. The steady build-up of inconsistencies within the prevailing model has become unsustainable. An intellectual breakthrough is conceivable once we have begun to discern the outlines of an alternate worldview. This prospect does not, despite the gloomy forebodings often broached, entail any return

---

6. Thomas Nagel has argued forcefully for "a major conceptual revolution" that would address the inability of science to account for itself in a mindless universe. *Mind and Cosmos: Why the Materialist Neo-Darwinian Conception of Nature Is Almost Certainly False* (New York: Oxford University Press, 2012).

to premodern patterns of discourse. One does not have to be a fundamentalist to concede the limits of a materialist outlook. Nor does one have to jettison the enlargement of rationality that the advent of modern science has introduced into our understanding of the universe. What is needed is a willingness to follow the thread of reason more deeply. The courage to entrust ourselves to the sustaining power of science itself can carry us beyond the impasse into which it has temporarily led us. A science that yields a view of the world that has no place for science itself is stunningly at odds with all that we know. Nothing is to be gained from refusing to concede the contradiction. However we begin to reconcile the activity of mind with a world that is explained largely in terms of its material components, nothing is to be gained by persisting in the attitude of denial. Obstinacy cannot disclose the way forward. Only a readiness to expand the horizon of our thought can accommodate the divergent implications within it. Somehow they must be compatible within a whole. It was that faith that has sustained the great enlargement of understanding that modern science has made possible. This is hardly the moment to renege on it for the sake of preserving an orthodoxy that daily becomes more threadbare. We must be willing to admit that science itself is at odds with the world-view it has constructed.

## *Science is a spiritual reality*

That concession is sufficient to inaugurate a turn away from it. Far from betraying the scientific advance, this entails a fuller commitment to its unfolding. Science must now begin to include itself within its purview. It can no longer limit itself to the material universe in order to find a basis for itself. The model of physical causation is simply not adequate to the thought world of science itself. Even if neuroscience were to comprehensively map consciousness within the brain, that would still not provide any access to what consciousness contains. It would be like looking at a house from the outside without having any intimation of what is going on within it. No doubt much useful information could be accumulated by such an enterprise. We might even be able to formulate general patterns of activity. But their meaning would entirely escape us. For that we would have to enter into the life world of the residents, questioning them as to their intentions and in the process revealing ours to them. Human society can only be known from within it. The same is true of the great enterprise of science it has generated. Science can only be understood in its own terms. Not even neurophysiologists communicate their thoughts in the form of brain events. They know their theories are intelligible only as thoughts. Of course there are physical correlates to what occurs in the mind, but that is very different from the assertion of an identity. Science, we must admit, is essentially a non-physical event in the sense that it can be accessed only in terms of thinking it. Just as science is not reducible to neurological phenomena, so it is not containable within the physical means of its communication. Science is no more in brains than it is in books. The marks or traces that scientific inquiry leaves behind are intelligible only within the minds that created them. Its collaborative aspect is primarily a meeting of minds.

That is an event that can occur anywhere and anytime because it occurs nowhere and in no time. While exploring the events of space and time science itself is definitively outside of both. There is no analog in the external world. Science is contained nowhere but within itself. Simply because scientists occupy space and consume food does not mean that their work can be identified with the evidence of their physical presence. From a biological perspective endless hours of attending to test-tubes, dials and texts is well-nigh incomprehensible. It is only because we too know something of its interior dynamic that it becomes intelligible. Strictly speaking science exists only within the minds of scientists. They do not even have to be in proximity to one another in space or time for that event to occur. Understanding leaps across the boundaries that confine us and endures forever. Even death does not destroy it for it can be accessed by all who come upon the record much later. What is preserved are not the marks on paper or a screen but the meaning by which they can be comprehended. Of course a physical means of communication is indispensable. Science does not work through telepathy. But its most decisive aspect is not the physical remainder but the meaning that lies utterly beyond it. If we did not know any better we would be inclined to say that science is essentially a spiritual reality and that scientists are spiritual beings. Even the term "spirit" however derives from the physiology of breathing. It suggests another kind of physical reality rather than another reality altogether. When pressed to name it, we can only say it is within us. Yet even that is not quite accurate since we are just as much within *it*.

The tropes of subjective and objective defeat us, as they must, when talk about them underlines their failure to encompass the real. All our thinking occurs outside the boundaries that might be assigned to it. The world of thought is certainly not subjective, but it is also clearly not in any way an objective reality. It is definitively within itself. We do not create it but find ourselves within it. The whole possibility of thinking arises from its primordiality that we can apprehend but not penetrate. We cannot think beyond the possibility of thought. It simply is, neither coming into existence nor departing from it. To think is to move within its eternity, although that does not mean that we become or comprehend the eternal. The mystery of thought is its transcendence of temporality. How that is possible we cannot really know because to do so would be to engage in the same transcendence. All that we can say is that it is the condition of the possibility of thought, just as it is the condition of the possibility of the person. The process is slightly more familiar in the case of the latter and may provide the best avenue on what thinking is. We know that persons present a persona, as the Greek origin of the word mask (*prōsopon*) indicates. The actor who holds a mask is not in the mask but has clearly gone beyond it. The whole of a person's life, all that they do or say, is not sufficient to disclose who they are, even to him or herself. In every revelation the person escapes revelation, as the inexhaustibility from which it derives. Yet we know it as such. The infinity that the person is cannot be named but it can be glimpsed, for that is the horizon within which all communication occurs. The person always says more than is said and reveals more than can be revealed. The uncontainable is contained for we encounter the other. Transcendence is the medium of communication. Science that moves within the same transparence is no stranger to the inaccessible. It can apprehend the order of things because it knows its own derivation from beyond it. This has nothing to do with belief in a divine origin or even with the aspiration for God-like comprehension we noted above. It is simply the transcendence of every limit that is the reality of thought. Even its own thinking is not outside of its purview, although it can glimpse that transcendence only obliquely.

Science arises from we know not where. Its beginning can be dated historically but not what provides the possibility of its beginning. That is the arc of the unsurpassable that Immanuel Kant was the first to clearly acknowledge. He saw that the epistemological quest for certainty was a dead end. Knowledge cannot secure itself without appealing to the same test of validity. Empirical verification cannot be empirically verified. What Kant did not discern so clearly is that his own insight is not so similarly afflicted. It is a grasp of the inexorability by which knowledge itself is grasped. Somehow his insight has managed to embrace its own ground. That is what the opening of knowledge always entails. It arises from the conviction that it must incorporate the means of its own success within its movement. Just as moral action includes the postulate of freedom, so scientific inquiry must include the postulate of intelligibility. The mind can understand and the universe can be understood. Nothing can empirically justify such faith which is both undeniable and indemonstrable. It is abyssal in the sense that it arises from a depth that cannot be plumbed. To call it a leap would be inaccurate for it is incapable of departing from its beginning, the intuition that it is in contact with the whole of being it inchoately contains. How could mind sever itself from what is innermost within it? The reliability of knowledge is not a conclusion to be reached but the basis by which it reaches out to the world. Nothing can confirm faith but faith itself. It is the movement by which all subsequent movement is sustained. Before it believes in anything, faith believes in itself. It is faith in faith. To say it is the horizon of thought is to create the impression that we know what it is. We are incapable of mastering it and stand instead within its radiance. The apprehension of truth, even a probable truth, cannot but acknowledge truth as such. We may, like Kant, be able to talk about categories of understanding but we cannot talk about the category of that discourse. We simply move within it.

In the same way, there is no science of science. There is only the transparence of the movement toward the truth and reality of things, a movement that exceeds any of the things to which it leads. Science, as Einstein so evocatively observed, is a bigger mystery to itself than any of the mysteries it seeks to probe. It is the comprehending mystery. That is why it resists scientific analysis, especially of the reductionistic variety that remains the default model. Not only is there no branch of science that operates as a form of mechanical causation, but science itself is the definitive refutation of the materialistic explanations it applies everywhere else. The "selfish gene" may be a scientific explanation but it is not an explanation of science. Nietzsche suggested that religious asceticism had migrated into the scientific asceticism of truth.[7] His point is commonly seen as a negative aspersion on the spirit of asceticism, but it could just as easily be taken as a more positive evaluation of science. For us science is the modern form of spirituality. It arises from an awesome dedication to truth, one that is willing to cast aside all that might provide comfort, including the comfort of illusion, for the sake of unwavering fidelity to truth. Even if science can find no higher meaning it can still preserve its unyielding commitment to truth. It would rather die without consolation than accept a consolation it knew to be false. Preservation of its integrity is sufficient reward for its struggle. When one thinks over Nietzsche's own commitment to the same struggle it is not clear that his remark is so disdainful. It may well be that he had hit upon the secret of modern science.

The resolute refusal of all consolation but truth may be its deepest impulse. When we ask whence this guiding conviction arises we must concede that it seems to come from far below the surface we normally inhabit. In many respects it emerges only from within its own logic. We know it cannot derive from scientific method since no method can be the source of its own initiation. A method is always adopted from outside of it. There must be something beyond the method that prompts its embrace. Faith in the method begins in faith itself. Nothing grounds it since nothing is prior to it. Faith is the sustaining movement that is the continuous unfolding of a beginning we

---

7. "All science . . . has at present the object of dissuading man from his former respect for himself, as if this had been nothing but a piece of bizarre conceit. One might even say that its own pride, its own form of stoical ataraxy, consists in maintaining this hard won *self-contempt* of man as his ultimate and most serious claim to self-respect. . . Is this really *to work against* the ascetic ideal?" *Genealogy of Morals*, trans. Walter Kaufmann (New York: Vintage, 1967), section 25.

cannot entirely fathom since we are borne along by it. All that we know is that it puts us in touch with a higher imperative than the merely biological. Life itself must be subordinated to its inexorability. Science in this sense is not only a transcendence of the spatio-temporal limits of our existence but arises from the same transcendence. Stephen Hawking's endeavor to supplant God within a theory of everything, including how everything came into being, is not so wide of the mark as its Promethean echo would suggest. It resonates with the very core of the scientific drive. Even God cannot be permitted to block the path by which we open toward the truth of all things. Like several modern mystics, it represents the determination to let nothing stand in the way of God, not even God himself.[8] The very intensity of this imperative discloses how far beyond science its interior impulse lies. Transcendence of all that might only satisfy, but not fulfill, attests to the unlimited openness from which it springs. Science at its deepest is the love of God. The challenge is to maintain the purity of heart required to put away the last vestige of ambition in the process. No hint of self-aggrandizement can taint it. The self itself is finally transcended in its acknowledgement that its self-transcendence is not its own. Only that which is transcendence can provide the condition of its possibility. Even the freedom of response is not properly its own, for it arises from it knows not where. Science with its soaring trajectory of all that *is,* is ultimately a gift that, like all gifts, can neither be claimed nor deserved. Perhaps it is in Hawking's own life that the life of the gift is most fully exemplified.

---

8.  "A method of purification: to pray to God, not only in secret as far as men are concerned, but with the thought that God does not exist." Simone Weil, *Gravity and Grace*, trans. Emma Crawford and Marion von der Ruhr (New York: Routledge, 2002), 20.

# 7

# Can it be Reasonable for a Scientist to Believe in God?

## William Reville

THE NOTION THAT BELIEF in God persists in the modern world only as a superstition inherited from pre-scientific times is frequently heard nowadays. Richard Dawkins, the well-known evolutionary biologist and spokesman for scientific atheism, argues strongly that, after Darwin's theory of evolution and in the light of modern science, it is irrational to believe in God, and any educated person who continues to believe is indulging in willful ignorance.[1]

I am a scientist and I am a Christian and I will argue that it is possible to be both without insulting reason. I will only speak about Christianity because I do not know enough about other religions to do them justice.

This article is structured as follows. I begin (section A) by comparing the bleakness of atheism with the hopefulness and balance of Christian philosophy. I then (section B) illustrate how Christianity has always valued reason and logic. In section C, I summarise some of the principal discoveries that science has made about the natural world, a world that bootstrapped its way from very simple beginnings to the complexity we see around us today. I next (section D) rebut Richard Dawkins' claim that modern science and, in particular, the theory of evolution through natural selection, has made God redundant. In section E, I discuss three questions that arise from a scientific consideration of the world and argue that one, not unreasonable answer to these questions, could be God. Finally (sections

---

1. Richard Dawkins, *The God Delusion,* London: Bantam Press, (2006).

F and G) I conclude that it can be reasonable for a scientist to believe both in science and in the Christian God.

## (A) Christianity and Atheism

The principal challenge to Christianity in the Western world today is atheistic humanism which claims that we can live and understand our lives satisfactorily on the assumption there is no God. It seems to me that this atheistic assumption offers a bleak outlook on life. On the other hand, Christianity offers a comparatively comforting outlook, one I believe that is worthy of consideration by anyone seeking an answer to the meaning of life. Of course I am not saying that one should choose Christianity because the atheistic interpretation of the human situation is uncomfortable. No philosophy can satisfy unless one is convinced of its truth on adequate grounds.

Atheism offers a tragic conception of human life. In the material world of the atheist, death is final. Our ultimate ideals and hopes can never be fulfilled, neither in our individual lives nor in the corporate life of the race (see section C). The mind-numbing misery suffered by so many throughout the ages is just a brute fact and neither the suffering endured nor the evil perpetrated can ever be redeemed or punished.

Bertrand Russell clearly spelled this out for the atheist in an early essay where he wrote:

> That man is the product of causes which had no prevision of the end they were achieving; that his origin, his growth, his hopes and fears, his loves and his beliefs, are but the outcome of accidental collocations of atoms; that no fire, no heroism, no intensity of thought and feeling, can preserve an individual life beyond the grave; that all the labours of the ages, all the devotion, all the inspiration, all the noonday brightness of human genius, are destined to extinction in the vast death of the solar system, and that the whole temple of man's achievements must inevitably be buried beneath the debris of the universe in ruins — all of these things, if not quite beyond dispute, are yet so nearly certain, that no philosophy which rejects them can hope to stand.[2]

---

2. Bertrand Russell, *Mysticism and Logic, and Other Essays*, London: Edward Arnold, 1918, pp 47f.

On the other hand, Christians believe that human beings are made for eternal life in a universe designed for the development of personal values. Christians view their lives in relation to a loving divine purpose and believe that purpose can create infinite good out of suffering, thereby justifying all the suffering that has been endured during one's lifetime. Christians also believe that one is accountable beyond the grave for evil one perpetrated in this life. This Christian claim is so big that it would seem to be irrational to dismiss it without critical examination.

## (B) Christianity and Reason

Atheists commonly describe religious faith as blind belief in the absence of evidence. Richard Dawkins does so in characteristically pugnacious manner: "It means blind trust, in the absence of evidence, even in the teeth of evidence."[3]

However, the fact is that the Christian Church always emphasized the importance of reason and evidence in the formation of faith. The Anglican theologian W. H. Griffith-Thomas (1861–1924) gave a commonly accepted definition of faith as follows: "Faith commences with the conviction of the mind based on adequate evidence; it continues in the confidence of the heart or emotions based on conviction, and it is crowned in the consent of the will, by means of which the conviction and confidence are expressed in conduct."[4] The Catholic position is that faith tells us more than we can know by reason alone, but faith cannot contradict reason. Pope John Paul II taught that faith without reason leads to superstition and reason without faith leads to nihilism and relativism.[5]

The commitment of Christianity to reason is well illustrated by natural theology, which investigates the existence and attributes of God using reason and ordinary experiences, without appealing to divine revelation. The best-known natural theology argument to demonstrate the existence of God is known as the argument from design. Historically, this argument was

---

3. Dawkins, R. In: *The Selfish Gene,* Oxford University Press, 1999, p 198.
4. Griffith-Thomas, W. H. In: *The Principles of Theology,* London: Longmans, Green, 1930.
5. Pope John Paul II's Encyclical Letter, *Fides et Ratio (Faith and Reason)* (14 September, 1998)

developed to its highest extent by the Protestant clergyman William Paley (1743–1805).

Paley argued as follows in his book *Natural Theology* (1802). Imagine you are out walking and you pick up a small rock. You can explain the history of the rock by examining its features. You will notice it is geologically similar to the local boulders, having been dislodged from its parent rock by weathering. The marks and indentations on its surface can be explained by the weathering effects of wind and water.

You pass on and pick up another object—a pocket-watch. You open the watch and see the complex system of wheels, cogs and springs, interacting with each other and driving the hands around the face of the watch. Clearly this watch cannot be explained as the outcome of random natural forces, as was the rock. The watch is clearly designed—its intricate purposeful mechanism implies a designer.

Now, Paley said, look around at the living world. It is full of wonderful devices, many far more complex than a pocket watch, and each clearly designed to perform a specific function, e.g. the human eye. Such complex design implies a designer and the designer of such wonderful mechanisms must be superhuman. The designer must be God.

Paley's argument was very good given the extent of biological knowledge at the time. However it foundered later on the rocks of the theory of evolution through natural selection introduced by Charles Darwin and Alfred Russell Wallace in 1858. This theory explains how Paley's 'designs' arise naturally through the process of natural selection (section D).

While Christianity has emphasized logic and reason in the search for freedom and progress, nevertheless, the opinion is often expressed that the successful development of the western world over the past thousand years was achieved in large measure by overcoming religious barriers to progress. The American sociologist Rodney Stark has comprehensively rebutted the notion of religious barriers to progress in two ground-breaking works.[6] Stark points to the commitment to reason in Christian European culture, rooted in its rational theology, and explains

---

6.  Stark, R. *The Victory of Reason: How Christianity Led to Freedom, Capitalism and Western Success* (London: Random House Trade Paperbacks, 2006) and R. Stark, *The Rise of Christianity*, Princeton University Press, (1996).

how Christianity and its institutions were responsible for the most significant intellectual, scientific and economic break-throughs of the past millennium.

Finally, logic and reason are the hallmarks of science and a credible case can be made (8) that Christianity played a decisive role in the rise of modern science in seventeenth-century Christian Europe.[7] The Greeks were obviously very intelligent and the Chinese had a sophisticated culture well before Europeans did, but modern science arose only in seventeenth-century Christian Europe. The way Christians think about the world has four significant consequences—this is also true for Judaism and Islam. Firstly, Christians expect the world to be orderly because the Creator is consistent and rational. Secondly, because God created the world, it is worthy of study. Thirdly, the creation itself is not divine and therefore we are free to experiment on it. Fourthly, the Creator was free to create the world as He wished and in order for us to understand the world we have to investigate it by doing experiments on it. All these influences were present together in seventeenth-century Europe, providing the ideal intellectual environment necessary to spark the birth of modern science.

## (C) What Science Has Discovered About the World

The function of science is to discover how the natural world works and over the last 400 years science has made the most amazing discoveries (9) as detailed below.[8] Science holds most of this knowledge securely, but some things are known only in principle:

- The world began about 14 billion years ago in an explosion of energy called the Big Bang and has been expanding outwards from this point of origin ever since.

- As the universe expanded, it cooled and the various forms of matter 'froze out'.

- There are 92 different elements in the world. The two lightest elements, hydrogen and helium, were formed in the Big Bang and the remaining 90 elements were later forged in stars.

7. Polkinghorne, J. *Quarks, Chaos and Christianity*, London: Triangle Press, 1997.
8. See Rerrris, T. *The Whole Shebang: A State of the Universe Report,* London: Weiderfeld and Nicolson, 1997.

- As the universe expanded, hydrogen gas clouds coalesced ever more tightly under gravity until eventually the hydrogen atoms were bunched so close together that they began to fuse together to form helium (nuclear fusion), releasing much energy in the process, and so the stars were born.

- Elements heavier than helium are bred in stars in complex fusion events. All life is based on the element carbon and every atom of carbon in the human body was made inside stars. We are literally made of 'stardust'.

- Stars die when much of their hydrogen is used up in fusion. Some stars become unstable and explode (supernovae) as they die scattering their contents far and wide. The heaviest elements are forged in supernovae. The scattered debris can coalesce with other hydrogen gas to form new stars and the debris can also coalesce to form planets.

- Our solar system with its central star (the sun) and orbiting planets, including earth, was formed about 5 billion years ago.

- Life began spontaneously on earth about 3.8 billion years ago, probably as a simple single form. (Science assumes that life originated spontaneously but this has not been demonstrated for sure.)

- That simple single form of life evolved, new species of life arose and gradually changed into newer species, becoming extinct themselves. These newer species also gradually changed into other species again, becoming extinct themselves, and so on and on until we arrive today at the myriad forms of life that colonize every environmental niche on earth.

- Our sun will die about 5 billion years from now. As it dies, it will first expand into a red giant phase, engulfing the earth and burning it into a charred rock. All life on earth will be destroyed. This will be the end of the human race unless we have left by then to colonize another part of space.

- The universe continues to expand and will probably do so forever. Eventually all the stars will die and the temperature of the universe will drop everywhere to near absolute zero. No life will be possible in this barren wasteland—the 'heat death of the universe.'

- Four fundamental forces (gravity, electromagnetism, and the strong and the weak nuclear forces) determine everything physical that happens in the universe.
- Some of the fundamental scientific knowledge that has been discovered has been applied to make and to do useful things — science-based technology. The world now runs on science-based technology — computers, communications, etc.

Science can explain how the universe spontaneously bootstrapped its way from a simple explosion of energy in the Big Bang up to the complex world we see today. There is no need to invoke any outside agency, e.g. a Deity, to drive the process forward. Science can even explain in principle how the Big Bang itself could have spontaneously emerged from a vacuum. So, it seems that, if God created the world, He created a world that can make itself. This amazing fruitfulness of the basic fabric of the world raises a very interesting question (Section E).

*(D) The Theory of Evolution does not Make God Redundant*

The theory of evolution through natural selection was co-proposed by Charles Darwin and Alfred Russell Wallace in 1858. This theory is the central unifying theory in biology, without which biology would just be a vast collection of unconnected data.[9]

Biological evolution through natural selection works as follows. Variation naturally exists amongst the members of every biological community. Some variations allow the individuals bearing them to adapt better to their environment than their fellows who do not have such traits. This confers a selective breeding advantage on these individuals who will leave more offspring than those who do not have these traits. For example, swifter antelope will avoid predator lions better than their slower companions and will leave more offspring. Heredity will ensure that the next generation of antelopes is enriched in swifter antelope. Nature automatically selects (natural selection) for traits that confer a reproductive advantage — 'survival of the fittest'. Organisms and their parts consequently seem to be deliberately designed to work efficiently. They are indeed 'designed',

9. Ayala, F.J., *Darwin's Gift to Science and Religion*. Washington D.C., Joseph Henry Press, 2007.

but the design is effected naturally and unconsciously by natural selection.

For one reason or another mistakes trickle into the hereditary genetic material (DNA). These mistakes are called mutations. Mutations are often harmful, their bearers fail to reproduce and these mutations are eliminated. But occasionally mutations are useful and confer a procreative advantage. Such useful mutations are naturally selected and spread through the population. Mutations trickle novel information into the system and are essential to the evolutionary process. A species slowly and gradually changes over time and eventually, over millions of years, the small changes accumulate to such an extent that a new species emerges.

The theory of evolution through natural selection overturned Paley's argument from design outlined in section B. However, the hypothesis that there is a God is not disproved because one particular supporting argument turns out to be wrong. There are other powerful arguments and ways of thinking about this question that are not overturned by the theory of evolution (section E).

A modern argument from design called intelligent design (ID) was formulated in 1989. In principle the ID argument is identical to Paley's argument except that the 'designs' in question now are complex molecular machines that exist within cells. The proponents of ID claim that such molecular machines are 'irreducibly complex' and could not have arisen through gradual Darwinian evolution. This argument has been comprehensively demolished by mainline science.[10]

I described in section C how the universe spontaneously unfolded from its simple beginning into the complex world we find today. Some scientists argue (section E) that this unfolding was a special case with regard to its consequences for the origin and evolution of life. This opens the possibility that the universe is rationally designed at a very deep level and, specifically, that the manner in which biological evolution works serves a plan.

Convergence is a well-known phenomenon in evolution, where a number of organisms that are evolving along entirely

---

10. See Miller, K.R. *Finding Darwin's God: A scientist's search for common ground between God and Evolution.* Harper Perennial, 2007 and W. Reville, "Intelligent Design", *Studies.* Vol. 96 (2007), pp 257–270.

separate lines independently come up with the same solution to a problem, e.g. the best design for an eye. The human camera type eye has been independently evolved at least 6 times in widely different organisms, e.g. in the human and in the octopus. The evolutionary palaeobiologist Simon Conway Morris likens all of the space (possibilities) that might be available to evolution to a vast ocean, but demonstrates that, in practice, evolution inhabits only certain islands in this ocean—islands of 'optimum design'.[11] He concludes that, although evolution is not rigidly constrained as to the details of the designs it achieves, it is constrained to move in certain general directions. For example, although it was not inevitable that human beings would have evolved with five-digit hands and feet, Conway Morris argues that it was inevitable that intelligent self-aware animals would evolve. The world seems to work to a deep-laid plan. Christians believe that this plan is the will of God.

Evolution through natural selection seems to be the most efficient way to generate the maximum range of biological possibilities that are then sieved through natural selection to produce the design that works best in the world. It is not a random process but a mixture of chance (genetic mutations and natural variation) and necessity (sieving of the range of possibilities through the mesh of the laws of physics that operate in the environment). Indeed this approach is used in engineering design as the most efficient to come up with an optimum design—a popular approach in designing new aircraft wings is to randomly vary the design parameters to generate a wide variety of possibilities and then to sequentially computer test each one.

Prior to the theory of evolution, Christianity had accepted the story of creation as outlined in the Book of Genesis, which says that the world was created by God about 6.5 thousand years ago and at that time God created all biological species in more or less the forms we see today. Mainline Christianity was initially taken aback by the theory of evolution, but came to terms with it relatively quickly. For example, the noted American botanist Asa Gray (1810–88) was a committed Christian. He provided Darwin with data on flowers that Darwin found helpful in developing his theory and Darwin valued Gray's opinion greatly.

---

11. Simon Conway Morriss. *Life's Solution: Inevitable Humans in a Lonely Universe.* Cambridge University Press, 2003.

Gray argued that God's plan for nature was realized through natural selection. Darwin was unable to share Gray's conviction but he did acknowledge in a letter to John Fordyce, May 7th 1879 that—"it seems absurd to me to doubt that a man may be an ardent theist and an evolutionist."

Many eminent evolutionary biologists believe in the Christian God; for example,Theodosius Dobzhansky (1900–75), a Christian of the Eastern Orthodox Church, led the twentieth-century neo-Darwinian synthesis that explained the theory of evolution in modern genetic terms. I have already mentioned Simon Conway Morris (1951–) in section C, and Francis S. Collins (1950–), leader of the public human genome project, is a devout Christian who wrote a book reconciling his faith and his science.[12]

And so, Richard Dawkins' assertion that no educated person can honestly be a theist in light of the theory of evolution is answered not only by the arguments of many Christian scientists but also by the formulator of the theory of evolution, Charles Darwin himself.

### (E) Three Questions that Arise out of Scientific Consideration of the World

Christians believe that God created the world. It would not therefore seem unreasonable to a Christian that the creation would bear marks of its creator. Does scientific examination of the world reveal such marks? Obviously there is no strong evidence of this sort or you would not have to wait on me to reveal it. There is little or no empirical evidence that God exists and, to be fair about it, this is a substantial point in favor of the agnostic and atheistic positions. Nevertheless, a scientific consideration of the world raises certain interesting questions—questions to which, *going beyond science*, one not unreasonable answer could be God. These questions and considerations scarcely constitute empirical evidence, they are little more than straws in the wind. Yet, for many, they are straws that blow, however tentatively, in the direction of God.

---

12. Collins, F.S. *The Language of God: A Scientist Presents Evidence for Belief.* New York, Free Press , 2006.

The three most important questions relate to the comprehensibility of the world, the fruitfulness of the basic fabric of the world and the striking suitability of the world for life.

## Why is the World Comprehensible?

The great scientists who laid the foundations of modern science were fond of saying that reality is written in two great books, the book of God (the Bible) and the book of nature. The book of nature is written in the language of mathematics as Galileo Galilei famously wrote in his book *The Assayer* (1623) — "Philosophy is written in that great book which is ever before our eyes — I mean the universe — but we cannot understand it if we do not first learn the language and grasp the symbols in which it is written. The book is written in mathematical language and the symbols are triangles, circles and other geometrical figures, without whose help it is impossible to understand a single word of it; without which one wanders in vain through a dark labyrinth."

Why is mathematics so successful in describing the world? Mathematics is a product of the human imagination. It is pattern-making. Mathematicians sit alone and think up patterns and relationships between patterns. When they have figured out certain patterns and relationships between them they express this in a shorthand form called an equation. When more than one equation compete together to be picked as the correct option, the most beautiful equation almost always turns out to be correct.

When the mathematician turns and looks out the window at the universe, he/she sees these equations already out there written into the book of nature — into the fabric of the universe. This striking coincidence calls for an explanation. As Albert Einstein said: "The most incomprehensible thing about the world to me is the fact that it is comprehensible."[13] Why are patterns that are pure products of human imagination already embedded in the structure of nature? Christians believe that we are made in the image of God. This would mean that we can dimly understand God's thoughts, which could explain how

---

13. Vallentin, A. quoted in *Einstein, A Biography*, London: Weiderfeld and Nicolson, 1954, p. 24.

our mental pattern-forming processes can reveal the logic behind the basic structure of the universe. As the eminent mathematical physicist John Polkinghorne has said "The universe, in its rational beauty and transparency, looks like a world shot through with signs of mind and, maybe, it's the capital M mind of God we are seeing."

## Why is the basic fabric of the world so fruitful?

Science can explain how the world developed naturally starting from a vacuum that exploded at a point and in which hydrogen and helium were formed. The intense ball of energy expanded and cooled. The first stars formed as hydrogen coalesced under gravity and the remaining 90 elements were forged later in the stars. Planets formed and, on at least one, matter organized itself into life which gradually evolved into conscious life and finally self-conscious life (section C).

The world is made of matter and energy and these are inter-convertible according to Einstein's famous equation $E = MC^2$ (where E is energy, M is matter and C is the speed of light). Matter is basically made of a handful of subatomic particles called quarks and leptons. Four elementary forces act between these particles by exchanging other force-carrying particles called bosons. The four forces are — the strong and weak nuclear forces (cause quarks to stick together), the electromagnetic force (binds electrons in atoms) and the gravitational force (much weaker than the other three forces and only acts significantly between massive objects). These elementary particles and forces behave and interact together in ways described by the laws of physics (e.g. the inverse square law of universal gravitation).

How amazing then that such simplicity could organize itself to develop sequentially along the pathway outlined in section C. This handful of particles and forces eventually sparked into life, initially very simple, possibly a slime. But, this slime eventually got up and walked, became conscious, then self-conscious, talked, thought about its own existence and pondered its long 14 billion year history of development.

The second law of thermodynamics is probably the most fundamental law of physics. It states that disorder inevitably increases in a closed system (a closed system neither exchanges matter nor energy with any other system). Our universe as a whole is a closed system and its overall disorder is continuously increasing. But yet, there are pockets of high order in the universe called life. These pockets of life harness energy from the sun and use this energy to build and maintain their local high order. The second law of thermodynamics holds true for the universe as a whole, but life successfully works against this tendency locally by harnessing the energy of the sun. Eventually of course, all the stars will die, life will no longer be able to maintain itself and the second law of thermodynamics will have its final victory.

All scientists know this basic story of the development of the universe and the tremendous fruitfulness of the basic fabric of the world. Many just accept this as a brute fact that just *is* and have no wish to ponder any particular meaning behind it. For many other scientists however the fruitfulness of the fabric of the universe points to a deeper meaning. The astrophysicist, cosmologist, and prolific popular author Paul Davies is one of these and expressed himself eloquently in his address on accepting the Templeton Prize in 2007: "Are we then just an accident of nature, the freakish outcome of blind and purposeless forces, an incidental by-product of a mindless mechanistic universe? I reject that too. The emergence of life and consciousness, I maintain, are written into the laws of the universe in a very basic way... We are truly meant to be here."

## Is the world fined-tuned for life?

Scientific examination of the world reveals that if certain of its fundamental properties differed ever so slightly from the values and form they have, life would either never have arisen or, if it did, would never have evolved into anything interesting.

The fitness of the world for life is recognized in a scientific/ philosophical principle, the anthropic cosmological principle, formulated by theoretical astrophysicist Brandon Carter in 1973. The anthropic principles drily states – "What we can expect to observe must be restricted by the conditions necessary for our presence as observers." Thus for example, it is no surprise that the universe is 14 billion years old because it takes this long for stars to build enough atoms heavier than hydrogen and helium, elements essential for life, particularly carbon, the element on which life is based, and then, once life got started, a few billion more years were required for life to evolve intelligent observers.

Science has revealed that the values of many fundamental physical constants are perfectly suited for life. As far as we know, the values these constants have could have fallen out differently at the time of the Big Bang, but if their values differed ever so slightly from the values they now have, life would not be possible.

The constants include Planck's constant, the gravitational constant, the mass of the proton, the charge on the electron, etc. For example, if gravity was slightly weaker than it actually is either hydrogen gas would never have condensed tightly enough to initiate nuclear fusion and stars would never have been born, or else the fusion process would proceed too weakly to emit enough energy to support life on a neighboring planet.

On the other hand, if the strength of gravity were slightly greater than it actually is, fusion would gallop away so quickly in stars that they would quickly burn off their nuclear fuel and die young. Consequently, they would not radiate enough energy to a neighboring planet for long enough to allow life to evolve into anything interesting.

Scientists divide into two camps as regards their reaction to the anthropic principle (and in their reaction to the comprehensibility of the world and the fruitfulness of matter). Some are impressed and conclude that something is going on behind the scenes. Others either dismiss the anthropic principle as a mere tautology or else 'refute' the fine-tuning arguments that arise from the principle by invoking the multiverse hypothesis, as do, for example, Stephen Hawking and Leonard Mlodinow in their book *The Grand Design*.[14]

The multiverse hypothesis states that the universe we inhabit is only one of an infinite number of universes that arose shortly after the Big Bang. The laws of physics are different in each universe and because an infinite number of universes exist, probability dictates that some universes must have a combination of laws and physical constants that support life and we

---

14. Stephen Hawking and L. Mlodinow, *The Grand Design: New Answers to the Ultimate Questions of Life*. London: Transworld Publishers, 2010.

happen to live in such a universe. I am not persuaded by this argument and I will discuss the multiverse idea in section F.

Some eminent scientists who were/are impressed by fine-tuning arguments include Fred Hoyle (1915–2001), Freeman John Dyson (1923–) and Paul Davies (1946–). Fred Hoyle was a famous British astrophysicist who worked out many of the details of how elements are bred inside stars. Freeman Dyson, a theoretical physicist and mathematician, is famous for his work in quantum electrodynamics, solid-state physics, astronomy and nuclear engineering. Paul Davies is a physicist who researches in cosmology, quantum field theory and astrobiology. He is also a prolific and popular science writer.

Fred Hoyle was a tough-minded atheist but his confidence in atheism was badly shaken when he discovered the fine details of how elements are bred in stars. For example, life is based on the element carbon but sufficient carbon for this purpose would never have accumulated except for the presence of a very unlikely 'resonance' in the carbon atom. This is only one example of very many apparently fortuitous accidents and coincidences, each essential to the eventual origin of life, that occurred along the long history of the development of the universe. In this regard Hoyle said—"I do not believe that any scientist who examined the evidence would fail to draw the conclusion that the laws of nuclear physics have been deliberately designed with regard to the consequences they produce within stars."[15] And "A commonsense interpretation of the facts suggests that a superintelligence has monkeyed with physics, as well as with chemistry and biology, and that there are no blind forces worth talking about in nature."[16]

Again, Paul Davies can discern signs of design—"The very fact that the universe is created, and that the laws have permitted complex structures to develop to the point of consciousness—in other words that the universe has organized its own self-awareness—is for me powerful evidence that there is something going on behind it all. The impression of design is

---

15. Fred Hoyle, "The Universe: Past and present Reflections," *Engineering and Science* (November 1981), pp 8–12.
16. Fred Hoyle quoted in Paul Davies, *The Accidental Universe* Cambridge University Press, 1982.

overwhelming".[17] And John Freeman Dyson — "As we look out into the universe and identify the many accidents of physics and astronomy that have worked together to our benefit, it almost seems that the universe must in some sense have known that we were coming."[18]

On the other hand, there is no shortage of eminent scientists who are unimpressed by the comprehensibility of the universe, the fruitfulness of matter and by the fine-tuning arguments. They see the universe as a brute fact that simply *is*, underpinned by no meaning. Unlike Simon Conway Morris (section E), they see evolution as an entirely contingent process that, if repeated again, would almost certainly produce very different results to those we see today. As usual Richard Dawkins, the well-known evolutionary biologist, is memorable when he writes, "The universe we observe has precisely the properties we should expect if there is, at bottom, no design, no purpose, no evil and no good, nothing but blind pitiless indifference."[19] And Steven Weinberg, 1979 Nobel Laureate in physics, — "The more the universe seems comprehensible, the more it also seems pointless."[20]

## (F) Is it Reasonable for a Scientist to Believe in God?

The function of science is to provide natural explanations for the natural world, whereas the function of religion is to explain our purpose in life and to tell us how to live good lives. Explaining how the natural world works is not one of the functions of religion and science does not deal with the supernatural — science neither denies nor affirms the supernatural, it simply has nothing to say about it. Science is materialistic in its method but not in its philosophy and one certainly does not have to be an atheist or an agnostic to be a scientist.

If evolution and the discoveries of modern science in general argue so powerfully against the idea of God, as claimed by Richard Dawkins and others, you would expect that very

---

17. Paul Davies, *The Cosmic Blueprint: New Discoveries in Nature's Creative Ability to Order the Universe*, New York: Simon and Schuster, 1988.
18. Freeman Dyson quoted in J.D. Barrow and Frank J. Tipler, *The Anthropic Cosmological Principle* (Oxford, 1986), p. 318,
19. Richard Dawkins, *River out of Eden: A Darwinian View of Life*, New York: Basic Books, 1995, pp 131–132
20. Steven Weinberg, *Dreams of a Final Theory: The Search for the Fundamental Laws of Nature*, New York: Pantheon Books, 1992

few scientists would believe in God, but this is not the case. The most respected modern survey in this regard was carried in 1998,[21] replicating another well-known study carried out in 1916. The results show that 40% of all scientists believe in a personal God. The percentage of believing scientists in 1998 remained unchanged since 1916. And, although it doesn't prove anything other than that it is possible to do first class science while maintaining belief in God, most of the pioneers of modern science were Christians, many of them quite devout.

I am not saying of course that it is reasonable for a scientist to believe anything he/she likes in the religious sphere. Science has a reliable and proven method for investigating the natural world and if religion proposes an explanation for some aspect of the natural world that contradicts the scientific explanation, then a scientist must accept the scientific explanation, or else prefer an explanation from a source that has no competence in this area. For example, a scientist who is also a Christian should accept that the creation account as written in the Book of Genesis is simply a story with a moral.

The possible implications, *going beyond science*, of the three questions that arise from scientific consideration of the world (section C) resonate deeply with me and cumulatively, if hesitantly, point towards a deep-laid plan underpinning the universe. I am particularly impressed by the amazing fruitfulness of the basic fabric of the universe. In 1714 Gottfried Wilhelm Leibniz asked the deep philosophical question — "Why is there something rather than nothing?" I would extend this question by adding — "and why is this something so fruitful?" That basic matter could spontaneously transcend itself, not once (becoming alive), not twice (becoming conscious), but three times (becoming self-conscious) is, to my mind, awesomely impressive. I accept all that science reveals about the world, but, to me, some of the details revealed by science make the universe seem eerily fit for life. These hints emanating from scientific consideration of the world scarcely constitute empirical evidence. They are little more than straws in the wind, but, *going beyond science*, it seems to me that they blow in the direction of a universe designed at a very deep level.

---

21. E.J. Larson and L. Witham, *Nature* 386 (1998), pp 435–436.

I have explained why the theory of evolution through natural selection (section D) does not make God redundant as Richard Dawkins claims, and neither am I convinced that the multiverse hypothesis (section E) answers the fine-tuning argument. At best, the multiverse explanation is no better than the fine-tuned single universe explanation (arising out of the anthropic principle). However, I think the multiverse is a weaker explanation because we know for sure this universe we live in exists but we do not know that the multiverse exists. In the single universe situation we ask why the laws of physics randomly fell out to support life so perfectly. In the multiverse situation we must ask essentially the same question. Why do the laws of the multiverse generate an infinite number of universes, thereby guaranteeing that some/many will support life? The multiverse explanation offers no conceptual advance over the single universe/designer explanation.

Why is it that I and other scientists can see these 'straws in the wind', whereas many scientists, probably the majority, do not? I don't know the answer for sure. It might be argued that I want to see these signs, but I could argue back that those who do not see the signs do not want to see them. I cannot answer for those who do not see the signs but I am convinced that there is more to my position than wishful thinking.

Perhaps it is like an ambiguous drawing. One well-known example incorporates two faces — the face of a young woman and the face of an old woman. When I look at this drawing I first of all see the young woman's face, then the image flips to the old face, then back again, and so on. Many people have this experience, but some people only see one of the faces. Nevertheless, both faces are there. Because many don't see the straws in the wind that I see doesn't necessarily mean that these straws aren't there.

So far I have been talking about god in an impersonal manner — a God who created and designed the basic fabric of the universe but who doesn't necessarily take any interest in us as individual persons. However, the Christian God is a personal God who not only created the universe but who also loves each one of us and to whom we are encouraged to pray for help and guidance. Scientists generally find it more difficult to believe in a personal God than to believe in an impersonal God.

It seems to me that one's attitude towards a personal God is determined by one's reaction to the person of Jesus Christ as described in the New Testament. If this Jesus strikes you as sane, if the story of his life and the content of his teachings stake a claim on your head and your heart, and if you find that abiding by the teachings of Jesus brings the peace and joy into your life that he promises, then it is as reasonable for you to accept the word of Jesus about God, with whom he claimed to be in close and constant communication, as it is for you to accept the word of any tried and trusted friend about some matter of which you have no direct experience yourself.

But, of course, if you think Jesus was delusional and/or you think his teachings are wrong and find they do not work for you, then it would not be reasonable for you to accept the word of Jesus about the existence of God.

## (H) Concluding Remarks

My purpose in this article is to illustrate that it can be reasonable for a scientist to believe in God. This is a different thing to demonstrating beyond reasonable doubt that God exists. Such a demonstration would require a very high standard of evidence, trumping all the evidence and arguments made by atheism and from which one can infer an overwhelming probability that God exists.

Claiming that a belief is reasonable requires a less rigorous standard and need not necessarily imply that the opposite belief must be false. For my part, I do not claim that atheism is necessarily an unreasonable position. I do not claim that atheism has no evidence or 'straws in the wind,' to support its position. I do feel however that atheism is not seeing the full picture. For their part, atheists will claim that I am seeing too much in my picture. I concede that atheism can be a reasonable position for those who genuinely see no 'straws in the wind' when they look at the scientific picture of the universe and who are genuinely unimpressed by the life and the teachings of Jesus Christ. On the other hand I expect the atheist to accept that belief in God is reasonable for a scientist such as me when I genuinely believe that I see signs of an underlying plan in the details of the universe and I am genuinely impressed by Jesus Christ.

# 8

# Striving Towards the "Omega Point" Henri de Lubac on Pierre Teilhard de Chardin

Noel O'Sullivan

A STUDY OF THE RELATIONSHIP between theology and science must, inevitably, take account of the contribution of French Jesuit, Pierre Teilhard de Chardin (1881–1955). The name of this priest-scientist looms large in the history of the religion-science debate. He was so convinced by the hypothesis of biological and cosmic evolution that he claimed the Church's insistence on denying it would amount to another Galileo affair. In 1922 he was forbidden to publish such views and spent most of his life in China working as a paleontologist, while continuing to be a committed Jesuit. During his time in China he was associated with the discovery of *Sinanthropus pekinensis*, a discovery of human origins that took place between 1929 and 1937. This was a major find, establishing that *homo erectus* was between 300,000 and 500,000 years old.

Born in the Auvergne region of France, Teilhard was drawn to the rocks in the mountains around his home from his earliest years. Thus began his fascination with nature, leading him to become a geologist and paleontologist in later life. In addition to his love of nature and the hardness of matter, Teilhard was drawn to the spiritual. He loved God and he loved creation. In his own words, he tried to discover "how... we can reconcile, and provide mutual nourishment for, the love of God and the healthy love of the world, a striving towards detachment and a striving towards the enrichment of our human lives."[1] As a

---

1. Teilhard de Chardin, *Le Milieu Divin* (London: Fontana, 1964), 53. French

young man he struggled to make sense of his dual attractions: his love of matter and his love of the spiritual. His spiritual journey led him to join the Jesuits, without having to sacrifice his other love; his superiors wisely encouraged his interest in science and he went on to take a doctorate in paleontology at the Sorbonne in Paris. And so he was destined to live his Jesuit vocation as a geologist and paleontologist.

This chapter attempts to open up the complexity of the man and his thought as he struggled to bring together the evidence of science and the truth of Christian revelation. This was a herculean challenge if we consider the context in which he was writing. Science continued to be viewed with suspicion from a Church perspective throughout Teilhard's lifetime. The encyclical *Humani Generis* was issued by Pope Pius XII in 1950, five years prior to Teilhard's death. This official document rejected the possibility of reconciling the *hexameron* (six day creation story in Genesis) and the claims of contemporary science in regard to evolution.[2] A careful cleric would hang up his scientific boots, but not so this passionate *Auvergnat*. Here we shall outline his attempt to reconcile a scientific world view with Christianity. We shall attempt to critique his system from both scientific and theological perspectives, taking account of the fact that Teilhard himself was not a theologian. We shall rely for our theological analysis on the writings of his Jesuit contemporary, Henri de Lubac, who wrote extensively on Teilhard's work. This will lead us to draw some conclusions about the work of this priest-scientist and enable us to answer the frequently posed question: is Teilhard still of relevance in the theology-science debate?

In evolutionary terms, Teilhard proposed creation as an ever-increasing process of complexification (not to be identified with multiplicity), beginning with the Geosphere (the earth), moving through the Biosphere (non-human life) and reaching its highest complexity in the Noosphere when human life appears. The three stages then were matter or earth (*geos*), life (*bios*), and mind (*noos*). This proposal raises hugely challenging questions: what is the relationship between these stages; does

original: *Le Milieu Divin* (Paris: Seuil, 1957), 28. The quotations from Teilhard's works are taken from the English translations. References to the French original are also given.
2. Pope Pius XII, *Humani Generis* § 5.

one give way to the other in an inexorable process of development? Teilhard attempted to answer this question in *The Phenomenon of Man*. He writes:

> In every domain, when anything exceeds a certain measure-
> ment, it suddenly changes its aspect, condition or nature. The
> curve doubles back, the surface contracts to a point, the solid
> disintegrates, the liquid boils, the germ cell divides, intuition
> suddenly bursts on the piled up facts... Critical points have
> been reached, rungs on the ladder, involving a change of
> state—jumps of all sorts *in the course* of development. Hence-
> forward this is the *only* way in which science can speak of a
> "first instant." But it is none the less a *true* way.[3]

According to the author each new stage in the evolutionary
process has its roots in a previous stage; in fact it exits in embryonic form from the very beginning. Teilhard calls this *cosmic
embryogenesis*.

He took the process a stage further to suggest that the final
unification of all things finds its completion in the Christosphere.
The law which governs the movement from initial multiplicity,
through greater complexity, to its goal in the One, the Omega
point, is the law of complexity-consciousness. By this he means
that as the universe moves externally to greater complexity this
is matched internally by a drive towards higher consciousness,
reaching its apogee in the Noosphere. Teilhard's method may
be described as phenomenological; he examines the structure of
the universe and reaches his conclusions on the basis of observable data. His is not the philosophical phenomenology of a Hus-
serl. While he observes the increase in consciousness that takes
place in tandem with greater complexity in the external world,
he does not delve into what we would term "psychological phenomenology." We could term Teilhard's method as "scientific
or material phenomenology."

This leads us to posit Teilhard's Christian interpretation of
his evolutionary world view. The process is put in motion and
brought through its different phases to its final unity by a divine
Omega, which Teilhard identifies with Christ.[4] In other words,

---

3.   Teilhard de Chardin, *The Phenomenon of Man* (London: Fontana, 1965), 86;
     French original *Le Phenomène Humain* (Paris: Seuil, 1955), 78.
4.   Pierre Teilhard de Chardin, *Mon Univers* (1924), IX, 85–6. Quoted in Gustave

Christ, through whom everything was created, is attracting the universe to its final destiny in Him. In this way Teilhard gives a Christian understanding of evolution, identifying its goal as the recapitulation of all things in Christ (Eph 1: 9–10). Thus Teilhard's system is future orientated; his concern is the *telos,* the end. He consolidates his *cosmic embryogenesis,* mentioned above, by invoking the Christian understanding of creation. In this way he dovetails science and Christianity. It is important to record that despite his interest in origins, Teilhard's theology of creation is more about the future than the past. His Jesuit colleague and friend, René d'Ouince, draws attention to the originality of Teilhard's anthropology by pointing out that it emphasises man's responsibility for the future of the world, with a new awareness of his power in that regard.[5] We now set out to analyze how successful Teilhard has been from the perspective of science and of theology.

*A Scientific Critique*

His major contribution from a scientific perspective is his acceptance of an evolutionary world view, a concept that was a daring hypothesis in his time, as we have seen. Nowadays, of course, it is accepted as a fact and, while it cannot be verified by a scientific experiment, no serious scientist would reject it. In this regard Teilhard was ahead of his time, especially as a Churchman. In his enthusiasm to embrace an evolutionary world view, he created several neologisms, which we have been using above: noosphere, christophere, cosmogenesis, etc. With these new terms he presented an understanding of evolution that is mesmeric. His language slips easily from that of science to poetry and, as such, is seductive. This tendency to move from one literary genre to another undermines his credibility as a scientist. Not surprisingly, he has met great opposition for his sometimes presumptions and unfounded claims, especially his claim that the later stages of evolution are present in embryonic form in earlier stages. One of his foremost critics

---

Martelet, *Teilhard de Chardin, prophète d'un Christ toujours plus grand* (Bruxelles: Editions Lessius, 2005), 38.

5. René d'Ouince, *Un prophète en process* tome 1 (Paris: Aubier, 1970), 16. Reference in François Euvé, 'Réflexions sur l'anthropologie de Teilhard de Chardin,' *Etudes* (Mai 2005), 634.

is Peter Medawar (1915–87) whose review of *The Phenomenon of Man* in 1961 amounted to a ridicule of this poet-scientist. He regards Teilhard's arguments as "fatuous," his discourse as "a willful abuse of words," and his work "a bag of tricks." He dismisses what he calls this "philosophy-fiction."[6] Sir Peter was a British biologist, born in Brazil, who was awarded the Nobel Prize in 1960. Such a negative critique from a scientist of his standing undermines Teilhard's scientific reputation. Our thesis here is that, while he overstepped his competence and drew conclusions not justified by the available evidence, Teilhard was pushing the boundaries of science in an attempt to present a complete system. In this he went too far. He tried to do likewise from a theological perspective and this was equally problematic, as we shall now see.

*A Theological Critique*

To open up a theological perspective on Teilhard we will examine three questions which have been the subject of controversy and which have cast a shadow over his standing as an "authentic witness of Jesus Christ,"[7] to quote a designation attributed to him by Henri de Lubac. The three questions are, firstly, his understanding of *creatio ex nihilo,* secondly, the charge of immanentism and, thirdly, the status of Christ as Redeemer. In discussing the first two questions we shall rely on the insights of Henri de Lubac who has written extensively on Teilhard.[8] For the third question we shall draw on the idea of the primacy of Christ in the Medieval tradition and as interpreted by Karl Rahner.

---

6. Peter Medawar's review of *The Phenomenon of Man* in the journal *Mind* (January, 1961) is republished in *The Art of the Soluble* (London: Methuen, 1967), 71–81. http://vserver1.cscs.lsa.umich.edu/~crshalizi/Medawar/phenomenon-of-man.html Accessed 26 June, 2013.

7. See *infra,* note 19.

8. Henri de Lubac, *La Pensée religieuse du Père Teilhard de Chardin* (Paris: Aubier-Montaigne, 1962; Paris: Cerf, 2002. English translation: *The Religion of Teilhard de Chardin* (New York: Image Books, 1968); *La Prière du Père Teilhard de Chardin* (Paris: Fayard, 1964); *Teilhard, missionnaire et apologiste* (Toulouse: Prière et Vie, 1966); *L'Eternel féminin, étude sur un texte de Teilhard de Chardin,* suivi de *Teilhard et notre temps* (Paris: Aubier-Montaigne, 1968); *Teilhard posthume, réflexions et souvenirs* (Paris: Fayard, 1977).

## Creatio ex nihilo

In his early writings (1916–20), Teilhard proposed a radically new understanding of *creatio ex nihilo*.[9] The 'nothingness' from which God created was 'pure multiplicity,' which has no existence. Creation was then a continuous movement from pure multiplicity to unity, the creative act being a process of unification for which he coins the word, 'cosmogenesis.' De Lubac sums up his position thus: "The pure Multiple will be conceived rather as a pure 'power of dispersion' which creation would have the function of 'reversing'."[10] Teilhard claims multiplicity gives way in the course of the evolutionary process (the cosmogenesis) to the One. The source of his understanding of the 'One' is not clear. Obviously, we are familiar with the idea of the One from Plotinus in third century Alexandria, which he connects to the idea of the Good. However, for Plotinus, and subsequent commentators, these are metaphysical ideas and Teilhard does not deal with metaphysics in his system; his theories are drawn from the physical sciences. The 'cosmogenesis' achieves its ultimate completion in the *omega* point, which Teilhard identifies with Christ.

However, some of the great merits of his work should be pointed out, in particular, his motivation to make sense of evolution from a Christian perspective. His system has the merit of being Christocentric, giving due recognition to the universality of Christ and the importance of the Eucharist in the state of becoming of the universe.[11] Everything begins and ends with Christ in his view. The influence of the first chapters of Colossians and Ephesians is evident.

What can readily be said of de Lubac's reaction to Teilhard de Chardin is that he understood him or, at least, he understood

---

9. The idea of creation *ex nihilo* is sometimes considered as having its origin in 2 Maccabees 7: 28, with the exhortation of the mother of the seven martyrs to her youngest son to withstand the wiles of Antiochus. See Romans 4: 17. See Origen, *De Principiis* II, I, 5, SC 252, p. 245. The doctrine of *creatio ex nihilo* was formally defined at the Fourth Lateran Council in 1215, DS 800. It was reaffirmed in the Vatican I document *Dei Filius*, DS 3002.

10. Henri de Lubac, *La Pensée religieuse du Père Teilhard de Chardin*, op.cit., 284. English text, 229. The quotations from de Lubac's works are my translation. References to the official English translations are cited where possible.

11. See, for example, 'Mass on the World,' in Teilhard's *Hymn of the Universe* (London: Collins/Fontana, 1970). French original: *Hymne de l'Univers* (Paris: Seuil, 1961).

what he was trying to do. Fourteen years his junior, de Lubac treated the older man with great sensitivity and sympathy. He recognized that Teilhard was a man of deep Christian faith who was earnestly seeking the truth in the context of a radically changed cosmological understanding. He recognized too that his fellow Jesuit was not a theologian but, rather, a scientist and poet. It is interesting that he entitles one of his books *La Pensée religieuse du Père Teilhard de Chardin* and not *La théologie du Père Teilhard*; in that he was correct.

In relation to the question raised by Teilhard's interpretation of *creatio ex nihilo,* de Lubac gently suggests that his colleague was attempting a physical, experimental synthesis of a metaphysical concept. Teilhard was impatient with such a metaphysical abstraction and wanted to make it more accessible by suggesting a 'meta-experiential' interpretation.[12] In other words, he wanted to discover an historical and practical formula in which to express the developments of creation. Commenting on the convergence towards unity, de Lubac summarizes: "It does not claim to be a metaphysical doctrine, but 'rather a sort of empirical and pragmatic explanation of the Universe'."[13] De Lubac goes on to describe Teilhard's early attempts to explain his metaphysics of union—or his meta-experiential interpretation of union—as "sometimes a little laborious" and which ultimately were unconvincing. He expresses his reservations succinctly when he writes: "Perhaps at the start he had wanted... to unify everything in too simple and, so to speak, too physically accessible a synthesis."[14] This comment says as much about de Lubac as it does about Teilhard. In exposing the weaknesses and impossibilities of the latter's ambitions, he reveals one key aspect of his own vision. De Lubac consistently recognized the danger of insisting on synthesis. For this reason he favored the idea of paradox to save the complexity of truth. Sometimes it is necessary to hold irreconcilable differences in tension and avoid the temptation to reduce them to an accessible simplification. It was Ronald Knox who once said the truth is rarely found in extremes.

12. Henri de Lubac, *La Pensée religieuse du Père Teilhard de Chardin,* op.cit., 284. English text, 230.
13. Ibid., 286. English text, 230.
14. Ibid., 288. English text, 233.

More pointedly, de Lubac criticizes Teilhard's impatience to synthesize in two ways. Firstly, it led him to abandon at times a sense of distance in his haste to find a convergence. Secondly, and more seriously, Teilhard did not have the technical know-how that such a synthesis would require. In particular, he failed to appreciate that a complete vision would require an appreciation of the different levels of the functioning of our intelligence and the constitution of our being. In other words, there is a question mark over his ability to distinguish the different orders, for example between the natural and supernatural orders. De Lubac asks the pertinent question: "Did he have a strong enough sense of the disruption that the revelation of the supernatural mystery brought, this "paradoxical mystery" as Clement of Alexandria called it."[15]

It is important at this juncture to record this serious criticism of Teilhard. The attempt to reconcile science and Christianity by collapsing them into each other is neither desirable nor possible. Religion and science have two different methodologies which need to be mutually respected. The scientific understanding of the world is compatible with Christian revelation, but it is a step too far to force both of them into a system, as Teilhard tried to do. In the process he did no favors to either. This leads us to consider the second issue, the criticism that Teilhard's system left him open to the accusation of immanentism.

*Immanentism*

One of the serious criticisms levelled at Teilhard from a theological point of view is the accusation of immanentism. He is accused of not adequately distinguishing between God and creation. In his highly acclaimed work on Christ in Teilhard's system, Gustave Martelet admits that his fellow Jesuit has spoken of a third, cosmic nature of Christ and of a 'new incarnation'. Fr. Martelet confesses that this is not very felicitous theologically but finds it acceptable as part of Teilhard's intuition which has not yet found a formula that is consistent with Tradition.[16] Martelet is here overindulgent in excusing what is clearly an unacceptable expression of the relationship between Christ

---

15. Ibid., 291–2. English text, 235.
16. Gustave Martelet, *Teilhard de Chardin, prophète d'un Christ toujours plus grand* , op. cit., 57.

and the universe. We now turn to Henri de Lubac's appraisal of the accusation of immanentism in Teilhard's writings.

In *La pensée religieuse du père Pierre Teilhard de Chardin* (1962), de Lubac poses a number of questions that arise, at least at the level of appearance, from Teilhard's writings. The most serious of these questions has to do with the place he accords to Christ in the evolutionary process. De Lubac summarizes his reservations thus:

> He wanted to show in Our Lord Jesus Christ the "synthesis of the created Universe and of its Creator:" has he not sometimes appeared to establish this synthesis at a level that is too accessible and so... more or less naturalises Christ?[17]

In Teilhardian terms, de Lubac wonders if he has not too quickly and *a priori* welded Christogenesis and Cosmogenesis. More strikingly still, he speculates if Teilhard has not perhaps drowned the unique given of the faith—the Mystery of Christ—in an ocean of a natural mysticism. De Lubac is careful to emphasise that Teilhard's writings give the appearance of these weaknesses and does not go so far as to say that they are necessarily justified but he does note that Auguste Valensin (1879–1953) expressed a more profoundly felt fear in this regard. In defense of Teilhard, de Lubac concludes that his colleague had opened up a great new idea which he himself (Teilhard) was not able to plummet. He quotes Cardinal Newman who claimed that mastering a new idea takes time.[18] Furthermore, de Lubac says that many of the Teilhardian writings which caused suspicion were undeveloped reflections which should not be used to condemn "an authentic witness of Jesus Christ."[19] We find here, as we did with Gustave Martelet, a conscious attempt to drag Teilhard into mainstream theological thinking.

In de Lubac's commentary on *Gaudium et Spes*, entitled *Athéisme et sens de l'homme* (1968), we find a more robust defense of Teilhard de Chardin and the charge of immanentism. De Lubac says, for example, that the charge of not respecting the transcendence of the Parousia, making it out to be somehow in mere continuity with terrestrial or cosmic reality, was not justified.

---

17.  Henri de Lubac, *La Pensée religieuse du Père Teilhard de Chardin* op.cit., 292. English text, 235–6.
18.  Ibid., 293, note 3. English text, 237, note 34.
19.  Ibid., 295. English text, 238.

To interpret Teilhard as saying that there is an indefinite development of earthly realities into a supernatural reality would be a deceptive and false interpretation of his writings. To divinize human progress would be to create an idol. Quoting from Teilhard's *Mon Univers*, de Lubac emphasises that the world is created for God and it "cannot come to God, *in Christo Jesu,* except by means of a total remaking where it seems to *disappear* altogether *without observable compensation* (in the terrestrial order)."[20] Salvation is only possible for the individual person and for the universe as a whole through a dying to self; this is the law of the Cross. The created order, no less than the human person, cannot be brought to completion without a re-creation. Teilhard's emphasis on rupture evokes the Pauline image of rebirth:

> From the beginning till now the entire creation, as we know, has been groaning in one great act of giving birth; and not only creation, but all of us who possess the first-fruits of the Spirit, we too groan inwardly as we wait for our bodies to be set free.[21]

In *Le Milieu Divin,* Teilhard expresses the dying and rising of creation as one of total transformation:

> Finally, by the crucifixion and death of this adored being, Christianity signifies to our thirst for happiness that the term of creation is not to be sought in the temporal zones of our visible world, but that the effort required of our fidelity must be consummated *beyond a total transformation* of ourselves and of everything surrounding us.[22]

To evoke Teilhard's language, the Noosphere does not transform itself into the Christosphere, but is transformed by "the personal and transcendent, the loving God:" "Only the personal and transcendent, the loving God, 'Centre of universal consciousness shining in the heart of Evolution, ... comes to save the muddled mass of the Noosphere from slavery'."[23] Against

20. Henri de Lubac, *Athéisme et sens de l'homme, une double requête de 'Gaudium et Spes'* (Paris: Cerf, 1968; republished in Œuvres complètes IV, Paris: Cerf, 2006), 407–514, at 501.
21. Romans 8: 22f, Jerusalem Bible translation.
22. Pierre Teilhard de Chardin, *Le Milieu Divin* op. cit., 103. French original, 106–7.
23. Henri de Lubac, *Athéisme et sens de l'homme,* op. cit., 502. De Lubac is here quoting Teilhard de Chardin, *Esquisse d'un Univers personnel* (1936, Œuvres, t. 6), 101.

the charge of immanentism and secularism, de Lubac defends his fellow Jesuit in these terms:

> He wanted to establish—and, we believe, he did so sure-ly—that without the sure hope of a transcendent order which eternalises us, but to which it is impossible to be introduced without passing through death, we would only be able to ut-ter a universal "what good is it?" [24]

There is no hope of continuity for the universe without rup-ture and without an act of God. Creation, no more than the human person, is not its own savior. The work accomplished by human activity is only a preparation for the Pleroma. To use another Teilhardian term, the entire process of 'hominisa-tion' is a preparation for the fullness of time. De Lubac quotes Jacques Maritain to summarize his own interpretation of Teil-hard's understanding of the relationship between the world and the Kingdom: "The world's coming to glory will not be the fruit of cosmic evolution, but the fruit of its transformation by an act of God." [25]

De Lubac's dialogue with the writings of Teilhard de Char-din provides a significant insight into his own understanding of creation and its relationship with the Parousia, an under-standing which eschews the pitfalls of Teilhard's writings. It is important to summarize de Lubac's vision of the relationship between Christ and creation as he makes an important con-tribution to the theology-science debate. The world created by God, and distinct from him, is the theatre and temple of his Presence. Created through the Word, the world is in con-tinuous dependence on Christ for its existence and evolution. Though present in the world, Christ is not a naturalized part of the world, something that would be akin to pantheism. Growth towards the Kingdom is not the fruit of a natural process in nature itself; rather it can only come about through the grace of God, though the human development of the world is part of the preparatory work. De Lubac's strongest point is the signifi-cance of the Christ event. Though anticipated in the scriptures as the fulfillment of the promises made by God, the coming of

---

24. Ibid., 502.
25. Jacques Maritain, *Le Paysan de la Garonne* (Paris, Desclée de Brouwer, 1967), p. 381, quoted in Henri de Lubac, *Athéisme et sens de l'homme*, op. cit., 503.

Christ is a unique irruption in human history. What emerges also in his dialogue with Teilhard de Chardin is the part that the logic of the Cross must play in the Christian vision. Both in human history and in the physical universe there is no transformation without death. New life, new creation comes about for humanity and for the cosmos through the process of death to self. This evokes the Johannine image of the grain of wheat.[26] There is continuity but, more strikingly, rupture in de Lubac's understanding of creation and its completion. For this reason we cannot give a precise description of the nature of the newness that comes about under the action of the Spirit. The universe too retains something of the imprint of its Creator and, as such, is marked by His incomprehensibility. Recognizing Teilhard's good faith in attempting to reconcile science with a Christian understanding of creation, de Lubac draws attention to the danger of a synthesis prematurely born. He did not make that mistake himself.

The essential point he highlights is the fact that the universe is an integral part of God's self-communication. God can be known through his works:[27] we can read him in the book of nature.[28] Yet God is distinct from creation and the summit of His self-revelation comes in Christ. So how does he justify his claim that we find the presence of God in the universe and that the whole cosmic reality is part of the final recapitulation of all things in Christ? De Lubac does not see his function as being that of finding solutions or parallels in the physical sciences, though he accepts Teilhard's attempts to do so. De Lubac's relies on Christology for his theological views on creation. It is because the universe is created through the Logos that there is something of His presence in creation and that it will be brought to completion in the recapitulation of all things at the end. It means that for de Lubac Christology is the key to interpreting creation. It enables him to express the unity between God and His creation and, at the same time, their difference. Without the Christological key creation would either remain a

---

26. John 12: 24f.
27. Vatican I, *Dei Filius* (1870), DS 3004.
28. St Bonaventure (1217–1274) describes the universe as a book: 'The universe is like a book reflecting, representing, and describing its Maker.' Bonaventure, *The Breviloquium* Chapter 11, 2, English translation by José de Vinck (New York: Tournai, 1963), 104.

mere shell having no connection with salvation, revelation and eschatology, or else it would fuse with the Godhead in a form of pantheism.

## Primacy of Christ

The third question which is significant in an assessment of Teilhard's vision is the place he accords to Christ as Redeemer. Gustave Martelet points out that Teilhard has moved the center of gravity of the Incarnation from being solely redemption from sin to being the creative act itself and our election in Christ before the foundation of the world (Eph 1:4).[29] At the time when Teilhard was writing, this Christological shift would have been regarded with suspicion. However, there is ample evidence in our tradition to support an understanding of the Incarnation as being primarily revelatory. Redemption is then seen as the secondary part of God's plan. We need to sift the evidence to support this understanding. In doing so we will see that Teilhard's interpretation of the Incarnation is justified. We begin with a quotation from Karl Rahner (1904–84).

In his essay "Christology within an Evolutionary View of the World,"[30] Karl Rahner draws attention to the Christological tradition associated with the "Scotist school," "which has always stressed that the first and most basic motive for the Incarnation was not the blotting-out of sin but that the Incarnation was already the goal of the divine freedom even apart from any divine fore-knowledge of freely incurred guilt."[31] Without in any way undermining the fact that the Incarnation of the Logos signifies the victory over sin, Rahner, in this essay, prioritises the link between the Incarnation and creation:

> In the Catholic Church it is freely permitted to see the Incarnation first of all, in God's primary intention, as the summit and height of the divine plan of creation, and not primarily and in the first place as the act of a mere restoration of a divine world-order destroyed by the sins of mankind, an

---

29. Gustave Martelet, *Teilhard de Chardin, prophète d'un Christ toujours plus grand*, op. cit., 37.
30. Karl Rahner, 'Christology within an Evolutionary View of the World', in *Theological Investigations* 5, translation by Karl-H. Kruger (Baltimore: Helicon, 1966), 157–192.
31. Ibid., 184.

order which God had conceived in itself without any Incarnation.[32]

Seeing the Incarnation as the summit of the divine plan of creation is a perspective that has far-reaching consequences. It recognizes the sovereignty of God to communicate His divine love in total freedom, not constrained by a new contingency resulting from sin. Rahner, in the article to which we are referring, has been influenced by Teilhard de Chardin. He refers to the reproaches pitted against Teilhard for seemingly rendering sin harmless, a reproach which Rahner accredits de Lubac with invalidating.[33] Though Rahner does not use the term, his essay on "Christology within an Evolutionary View of the World" finds its place within the "primacy of Christ" perspective. This term is based on the Pauline notion that Christ is "the image of the invisible God, the firstborn of all creation."[34] The idea of the "primacy of Christ" is found in Franciscan Christology to describe the predestination of Christ, a concept which we shall now explain.

This doctrine is especially associated with the writings of John Duns Scotus (c. 1266–1308), but its roots lie with Rupert of Deutz (c. 1075–1130), who affirmed that Christ would have become incarnate irrespective of the Fall. One reason for this affirmation is based on the principle associated with Dionysius the Pseudo-Areopagite, viz., that good is self-diffusive and the Incarnation represents the highest form of the self-diffusion of good. St. Thomas also endorsed this Dionysian principle when he expressed an understanding of the Incarnation as God's highest self-communication[35] though he did not endorse the view that Christ would have become incarnate irrespective of sin. For Thomas this was a hypothetical question best left aside because we can only know God's will from scripture and scripture clearly teaches that the Incarnation was willed by God because of the sin of Adam.[36] Scotus argues — but for reasons that

---

32. Ibid., 185.
33. Ibid.
34. Colossians 1:15.
35. St. Thomas Aquinas, *Summa theologiae*, III, q. 1, art. 1, resp.
36. Ibid., art. 3, resp.

differ from those of Rupert of Deutz—that Christ would have become incarnate irrespective of the Fall.[37]

In the light of this survey of the possible reasons for the Incarnation we see that Teilhard's shift of the center of gravity from Redemption to the primacy of Christ does not compromise his position in the theological tradition of the Church. Understandably, in his time one can appreciate the unease his claims may have caused. But his belief in the Redemptive role of Christ was not something he compromised.

*Conclusion*

The writings of Teilhard de Chardin will always have an important place in Christian literature and for two reasons, in particular. The first reason is his insistence on the complementarity of science and Christian revelation. He himself lived the tension that frequently saw them pulling against each other and he did so in a most personal way from his earliest years growing up in the Auvergne. He refused to sacrifice his love of the universe to his love of God, and vice versa. In this his instincts were truly human and truly Christian. It also places him in the Thomistic tradition. St. Thomas Aquinas was keenly aware that the truth should be welcomed, irrespective of its source: "All truth, irrespective of who expresses it, comes from the Holy Spirit as the source of natural light and as exercising on the spirit of man a desire to grasp and speak what is true."[38]

However, Teilhard suffered for his beliefs, being forbidden by his Jesuit superiors from publishing his major works in his lifetime. Books like *The Phenomenon of Man* (1955) and *Le Milieu Divin* (1957) were published posthumously. He was regarded with suspicion for the reasons we have outlined above: his espousal of an evolutionary world view; the suspicion that he was 'weak' on sin and Redemption; the accusation of immanentism. Furthermore, his scientific synthesis did not stand up to the rigors of his discipline, though his paleontological work in China has stood the test of time.

Teilhard's pitfall was his insistence on bringing theology and science into a neat synthesis. Henri de Lubac rightly drew

---

37. See Richard Cross, *Duns Scotus* (Oxford: Oxford University Press, 1999), 127–132.
38. St. Thomas Aquinas, *Summa theologiae,* I, II, q. 109, art. 1.

attention to that weakness. He himself always allowed the mystery to dominate. Science and theology are different disciplines and need to respect each other's axioms and methods. Teilhard tended towards syncretism as he collapsed one discipline into the other. We look to science for knowledge of *how* the universe functions: theology is a discourse on the meaning of human existence; it answers the question, *why?*[39] Teilhard obviously labored under the disadvantage of not being a theologian or philosopher.

The second reason that will ensure a permanent place for Teilhard among the great Christian writers is that his writings are profoundly spiritual. In a review of several publications to mark the centenary of his birth, Donald Goergen highlights the spiritual heritage bequeathed by Teilhard.[40] His writings give hope and inspiration to people who experience deeply their rootedness in the earth and, at the same time, their spiritual patrimony. So much of our spirituality has been ethereal, with an unhealthy renunciation of God's creation. Teilhard and de Lubac have rightly accorded a significance to the cosmos that was often lacking in our tradition, when it was regarded as the disposable theatre or temple where salvation history unfolded. The universe will form part of the recapitulation of all things in Christ. Such an understanding of creation and its eschatological goal should give a theological foundation to a balanced ecology, a discipline often bereft of a sense of its source and end.

In a letter to Archbishop Paul Poupard, then Rector of the Institut Catholique in Paris, on the occasion of the centenary celebrations (1981), Cardinal Casaroli, the Secretary of State, wrote the following:

> Geared to the future, this synthesis, often so lyrical in expression and fraught with a passion for the universal, will have contributed to restoring to men tormented by doubt the taste of hope. At the same time, the complexity of the problems

39. The following definition of theology is difficult to surpass: 'Christian theology is the methodical study, within an existential commitment of faith, of the meaning and credibility of the self-disclosure in Christ of the supreme Mystery of existence.' Kevin McNamara, *Sacrament of Salvation: Studies in the mystery of Christ and the Church* (Dublin: Talbot Press, 1977), 25.
40. Donald Goergen, 'Current trends: Recent Studies of Pierre Teilhard de Chardin,' in *Spirituality Today* (Fall 1982, Vol. 34, N° 3). http://www.spiritualitytoday.org/spir2day/823436goergen.html Accessed 26 June, 2013.

tackled, as well as the variety of approaches adopted, have not failed to raise difficulties, which rightly motivate a critical and serene study—both on the scientific and on the philosophical and theological levels—of this exceptional work.[41]

While acknowledging the magnitude of Teilhard's work and the message of hope it gives to humanity, the letter also points to the difficulties arising from the work, both at the scientific and at the theological and philosophical levels. This is an apt summary of what this chapter has tried to achieve.

Finally, while we may legitimately have difficulty with some of Teilhard's theses and conclusions both in science and theology, we cannot deny his passion for the truth which these disciplines represent. His commitment and hard work are daunting. Inspired by this great grandnephew of Voltaire, it behoves us to imitate his engagement with God and his creation: *il faut cultiver notre jardin.*

---

41. Cardinal Casaroli, quoted in Donald Goergen, Ibid., par. 4.

# 9

# Do We Know Where We Are?
# Creation and the Trinity

## Brendan Leahy

SINCE DARWIN'S 1859 CLASSIC work on evolution, Christians have been called to clarify what they mean by their doctrine of creation. A common misunderstanding, as other contributors in this book have pointed out, is that the Christian doctrine of creation is a scientific teaching akin to physics. Perhaps some Christian writers have given this impression. Yet the notion of creation as indicated in Scripture and in the thought of classic theologians such as Thomas Aquinas is on a different level. Scientific studies about the beginning of our universe have provided much knowledge and important discoveries, but the Christian notion of creation opens a horizon that casts light on the existential questions to do with our origins and destiny as well as our ethical and ecological vocation. It is for this reason the Catechism of the Catholic Church reminds us that,

> Catechesis on creation is of major importance. It concerns the very foundations of human and Christian life: for it makes explicit the response of the Christian faith to the basic question that people of all times have asked themselves: "Where do we come from?" "Where are we going?" "What is our origin?" "What is our end?" "Where does everything that exists come from and where is it going?" The two questions, the first about the origin and the second about the end, are inseparable. They are decisive for the meaning and orientation of our life and actions (n. 282).

It is possible to list at least three distinct layers of meaning contained in the doctrine of creation. Firstly, it is a statement about God's generous "giving" of creation as gift. It affirms God's Lordship over all things. We didn't create ourselves. Rather, creation is an originating act of God by which he freely shares his being with what, in itself, doesn't exist.

Secondly, the Christian notion of creation refers to the "gift" itself, in other words, to the world/creation that is distinct from God, the fruit of his creative act. Here we are talking about the cosmos and humanity, that which has come about as a result of God's creative activity.

Thirdly, and this aspect is often neglected, creation can be spoken of in terms of the dynamic and continuously creative "relationship" that exists between God and the world. In other words, God didn't simply set up a world in the past distinct from himself, and then forget about it. He freely bestowed existence on creation with a view to bringing it into full communion with himself. Creation is already a participation in as well as being a project moving towards fulfillment in God. And all of this is taking place within God's continuing and creative providence.

In this short chapter I want to focus on the Trinitarian home and destiny of creation. Precisely as the transcendent Creator of all that is, God has placed everything in existence and *keeps* creation in being. He is always transcendent to and is not bound by any of the limits of this world. And yet, because of Jesus Christ, we know that our world has a home. It is embraced within the divine community of love and dialogue that is the Triune God, Father, Son and Holy Spirit, revealed to us in Jesus' life, death and resurrection. We already participate in, and are journeying towards, our fulfillment in a creation that will be fully set into the dynamic divine life of glory.

## Biblical Perspective on God's Creative Plan

The Bible speaks about creation at several points. In the Old Testament we find reference to it in particular in the Book of Genesis (chapters 1–9) but it is spoken of in other parts as well such as the Wisdom literature, the Psalms, and the prophetic writings (in particular in Deutero-Isaiah, 40–55). The New Testament takes it for granted that God created the world. For instance, we find references to the "foundation of the world" (Mt 25:34; Lk 11:50; Jn 17:24; Eph 1:4; Pet 1:20). What is new in the New Testament is the Christological focus as we shall mention below.

In its doctrine of creation, Biblical revelation wants us to understand creation as the beginning of a relationship between God and the world, a relationship that was dynamic and transformative, permeating all that is, a relationship that directed creation forward towards a future promise.

When the first chapters of the Bible speak of the primordial "chaos", they are not offering us vague, speculative thought about pre-existing matter alongside the Absolute such as to be found in theories found in Greek philosophers. Rather, the Biblical writers are presenting an existential message to us. It has to do with the struggle of good and evil. What they want to underline is that no matter how great the threat, the cosmos created by God cannot ultimately be contradicted. On the contrary, there is a dynamic in history. The cosmos has not yet reached its fulfillment, but its destiny towards accomplishment is embraced within God's loving accompaniment and covenantal plan. The way the Fall and expulsion from the Garden of Eden is recounted conveys the same message: the negative has to be understood within the merciful hope promised by God.

The new focus in the New Testament is the link between creation and the event of Jesus Christ, the Incarnate Word and Wisdom of God. While assuming the Old Testament revelation that indeed provides the framework for the Christ event, the New Testament writers are overwhelmed by something new that they realize has opened up with Jesus Christ, the divine-human Son of God. What they present to us is the belief that the Christ event that culminated in Jesus' cry on the Cross and his death and resurrection, resulted in a "new creation" (cf 2 Cor 5:17; Gal 6:15), that is, a deeper and more radical meaning of creation itself.

On the one hand, monotheistic faith is clear that creation is the gift of the "One" God praised three times a day by the people of Israel in the great prayer and statement of faith found in Deut 6:4–5: "The LORD is our God, the LORD alone. You shall love the LORD your God with all your heart, and with all your soul, and with all your might". But, on the other hand, in and through Jesus' life, death and resurrection, the first Christians

161

came to see creation as coming from the God who is not only One but also Triune, Father, Son and Holy Spirit. And this cast new light on the notion of creation, revealing much more about God's plan for creation and humanity.

From what we read in the New Testament, creation finds its home, as it were, in God who is Love. The world has been created "in Christ", and, in the power of the Spirit, is caught up in a dynamic of recapitulation of all that is, into the heart of God the Father. In the Prologue of John's Gospel, for instance, we read that "in the beginning was the Word and the Word was with God and the Word was God" (1:1). This Word (the Son of God) "was in the beginning with God. All things came to be through him, and without him nothing came to be." (1:2–3).

St. Paul too affirms that all has been created through Christ and in view of Christ and all subsists in Him. Christ represents the culmination of creation. He is the goal of creation. In the letter to the Colossians, we read a majestic statement about Jesus Christ and the cosmos: "He is the image of the invisible God, the firstborn of all creation; for in him all things in heaven and on earth were created... all things have been created through him and for him. He himself is before all things, and in him all things hold together" (Col 1:15).

Paul describes creation as "groaning in labor pains" (Rom 8:22–23) as it strives towards its fulfillment in Christ. In other words, the divergences that we see in the fractured nature of our world - with its natural disasters to the human divisions – are mysteriously converging on Christ with a view to an ultimate plan of unity in God. Paul writes, "When all things are subjected to him, then the Son himself will also be subjected to the one who put all things in subjection under him, so that God may be all in all" (1 Cor 15:28). In the Eschaton God will be all in all. God will be in his creation and the creation will be in him. The world will be totally penetrated by the glory of the triune God. God and the creation will be distinct but totally interpenetrated. Little wonder that, in view of this destiny that stamps creation, poets like Gerard Manley Hopkins can write "the world is charged with the grandeur of God."

*Reflection through the Ages on the Trinitarian Vision of Creation*

On the basis of rich Scriptural foundations, theologians through the centuries have reflected on the doctrine of creation. During the Patristic period they explored it by stressing the totally free action of God in creating and the universal extent of this divine action. They admired the goodness and harmony of the whole universe, created and preserved by the one God. The aspect of creation's dependence on God was highlighted.

The second century writer, Irenaeus, wrote that's there's a Trinitarian "rhythm" to the whole of creation. A favorite image of his is that of God's "two hands", the Son and the Spirit, involved in creating and organizing all things. In particular, the Trinitarian "rhythm" can be detected in the progress of humanity within God's project of creation:

> Such is therefore the order, such is the rhythm and such is the movement through which man, created and modelled, becomes the image and likeness of the uncreated God: the Father decides and commands, the Son carries out and models, the Spirit nourishes and grows, and man gradually progresses and is elevated towards perfection, that is, he draws near to the Uncreated; because only the Uncreated is perfect, and this is God... Because it is God who must be seen one day, and the vision of God procures incorruptibility, and "incorruptibility makes us near to God."[1]

For Irenaeus, creation finds its drive towards fulfillment expressed in humanity's journey towards union with God. Humanity is fully alive when it "sees" God. God's glory is humanity fully alive.

In his *Confessions* Augustine (374–430) provides us with reflection on the nature of time that begins with creation. In his major work, *The Trinity*, he describes how the universe bears the traces of the Trinity (*vestigia Trinitatis*). He invites us to open our mind to contemplation of our world created by the Triune God. The main trace of the Triune God is found in the human being. Famously, he proposed we can see an image of the Trinity both in our inner subjectivity as well as in the inter-relationship of lover, the beloved and love itself.

---

1.    Adversus Haereses, IV, 38:3

When it comes to asking what is it that permits the mutual indwelling of God in us and of us in God, he emphasizes the role of the Holy Spirit. He quotes 1Jn 4:13: "This is how we know that we remain in him and he in us, that he has given us of his Spirit" and continues, "So it is the Holy Spirit of which he has given us that makes us abide in God and him in us. But this is precisely what love does. He then is the gift of God who is love... So it is God the Holy Spirit proceeding from God who fires man to the love of God and neighbor when he has been given to him, and he himself is love."[2] Paul in his letter to the Romans, so often quoted by Augustine, also confirms this: "... the love of God has been poured out into our hearts through the holy Spirit that has been given to us" (Rom 5:5).

In the thirteenth century Thomas Aquinas distinguished the notions of "substance" (that which is in itself) and the "act of being" (the act by which all that is exists). Applying this to the doctrine of creation, he explained that since God is the Being who subsists of Himself, it is necessary that every other being is created by God, that is, every other being receives its act of being from God.[3] Aquinas stated that "creation isn't a change, but is the very dependence of created being on its beginning. It belongs to the category of relation."[4] For him to say the world is created means it exists in virtue of the relationship with God that places it and keeps it in being.

It was reflection on creation in terms of the relationship, in the Spirit, between Jesus Christ, the Word of God, and God the Father that enabled further reflection on the "place" of creation within the inner-Trinitarian relations. The Father gives away everything in love to the Son. The Son responds in perfect freedom to the Father. The love between the Father and the Son provides the "space" as it were for otherness and difference. This is the condition of possibility for creation to come into existence. God's love overflows, making room for creation and history, and this room is "in Christ."

It is in the light of their reflection on God's revelation in Jesus Christ that both Thomas Aquinas and Bonaventure understood

---

2.   *The Trinity* (New York: New City, 1991), XV, 31.
3.   S.Th. 1, 44, 2.
4.   *Summa contra Gentiles*, II, 18

creation as the extension outwards (*ad extra*) of the inner-Trinitarian relations of generation and spiration. Bonaventure wrote that God could not have created creatures by his will if he had not already generated the Son by his nature. Thomas Aquinas wrote that, "thus God the Father effects creation by his Word, who is the Son, and by his love, who is the Holy Spirit. Thus it is the processions of the Persons that cause the generation of creatures...."[5]

Jesus Christ is presented in Medieval theology also as the exemplary cause of creation. In other words, in him, the Word made flesh, not only has he brought about a new creation through his death and resurrection, but in him we see what creation is meant to be. The world is destined, through humanity, to share by grace in Jesus Christ in his relationship with the Father in the atmosphere of the Holy Spirit. As John O'Donnell writes, "the goal of creation is to be re-enfolded in the Trinitarian life."[6] This vision explains the structure of Thomas Aquinas' great work, the *Summa Theologica*. He presented the world in terms of its exodus from God and its subsequent return to him. Creation as the gift of God's creative action itself is far from being understood as inanimate raw material, but rather a living reality, charged with and bearing the stamp of God's own creative action.

The Age of the Enlightenment brought with it many developments in science, philosophy and theology. All of this impacted on the understanding of creation. The Trinitarian perspective evident in Thomas Aquinas and Bonaventure weakened. In its place we find a static notion of a mechanistic and determined universe. The focus on creation became limited to a consideration of the beginning of the world in a mechanistic sense. The specifically Christian perspective on creation faded. Christology was limited to reflection about Jesus' nature and redemption, the Trinity was abstracted to speculation about God in himself, and creation was explained primarily in terms of origins at the "beginning" in almost chronological terms.

---

5.　See 1 *Sent. prol.* quoted in Hans Urs von Balthasar, *Theo-Drama, V: The Last Act* (San Francisco: Ignatius Press, 1988), p. 62.

6.　O'Donnell, *The Mystery of the Triune God* (London: Sheed & Ward, 1988), p. 163.

With an increasingly theistic or deistic notion of God taking hold in Western culture, God came to be viewed as distant from the world. A dynamic relationship between God and the world was deemed impossible. The idea became popular that the world was simply like a watch wound up and set going by God but left to itself. Creation at best was now understood as a "product" that God the Creator, the First Cause, had set in motion but with which he now had no further link. Indeed soon the very notion of God was considered a threat to creation and to humanity. The world became increasingly viewed simply as raw material for human action. Creation ended up homeless, wandering without direction. Economic and social systems also lack a "home." This has negative consequences in that an authentic integral humanism requires an acknowledgement of the created nature of our universe because, "without the Creator the creature disappears."[7]

*Knowing Where we Are*

At the very beginning of modernity, the fifteenth-century Renaissance writer, Giovanni Pico della Mirandola, imagined God in conversation with humanity. It's a text that expresses the awesomeness both of humanity's created dignity and the radical call to shape our world:

> We have given you, O Adam, no visage proper to yourself, nor endowment properly your own, in order that whatever place, whatever form, whatever gifts you may, with premeditation, select, these same you may have and possess through your own judgement and decision. The nature of all other creatures is defined and restricted within laws which We have laid down; you, by contrast, impeded by no such restrictions, may, by your own free will, to whose custody We have assigned you, trace for yourself the lineaments of your own nature. I have placed you at the very center of the world, so that from that vantage point you may with greater ease glance round about you on all that the world contains. We have made you a creature neither of heaven nor of earth, neither mortal nor immortal, in order that you may, as the free and proud shaper of your own being, fashion yourself in the

---

7.   See the Second Vatican Council's document on the Church in the Modern World, *Gaudium et Spes*, 36.

form you may prefer. It will be in your power to descend to the lower, brutish forms of life; you will be able, through your own decision, to rise again to the superior orders whose life is divine.[8]

It can be said that humanity today needs to find its bearings if it is to order and shape the world that has been entrusted to it. There is no limit to the crises that our world experiences – from economic disarray to armed conflicts that leave us distraught; from ecological disasters to a globalization of technology that can leave us so "alone together" as the Chief Rabbi Sacks put it some years ago. One of the ways Christian faith can today help humanity to rediscover its bearings is to offer a renewed presentation of its doctrine of creation in terms of the Triune life of Creator God.

There is a new recognition growing that in the Christ event we see not only our redemption but also who God is in his own inner life and, in turn, who we are since humanity is created in the image and likeness of God. We also discover in the Christ event the place of creation in God's unfolding plan. At a time when science has moved from a static mechanistic view of the world to a more evolutionary understanding of our world, theology is offering new avenues of reflection based on Scripture and Tradition that speak to a dynamic worldview crying out for an adequate anthropology and cosmology.

Theologians from various Christian traditions have invited us to rediscover the significance of Trinitarian doctrine for our understanding of creation and anthropology. We can think of Catholic writers such as Hans Urs von Balthasar and Karl Rahner, theologians from the Protestant tradition such as Jürgen Moltmann and Wolfhart Pannenberg, the Anglican John Polkinghorne as well as the Orthodox theologians Dumitru Staniloae and Sergei Bulgakov.

One particularly stimulating line of reflection in theology is the invitation to revisit the ancient notion of "creation out of nothing" and read it in the light of Christological and Trinitarian doctrines for what it says about our world and how humanity is to play its role in co-operating with God. On the one hand, Christians see the doctrine of "creation out of nothing" as af-

8.    *Oratio de hominis dignitate*, 8–9.

firming the utter transcendence and freedom of God in creating. But we can also read this doctrine in the light of the event of the Cross as indicating the "how" of God's involvement in creation and our creative response to the Triune God.

It is in the mystery of the Cross that we learn that we and our world are caught up into a dynamic of love that originates in the relationship between the Father and Son, in the Holy Spirit. On the one hand, we see before us in the event of Jesus' death the culmination of the Son of God's "kenosis", that is, his emptying of himself to take on our human form right to the point of abandonment and death on a Cross (cf. 2 Phil 2:6–11). In this he is distinct from but utterly united in obedience to the Father. In a "nothingness of love" the Crucified Christ on the Cross, out of love, laid down his life (became small, limited, "nothing") for us and in this entered into the Resurrection. In this he showed us the key to reality. Love is the driving force of our world. The universe is undergoing what Teilhard de Chardin called "amorization."

Through the love made manifest in Jesus Christ, we learn to consider others greater than ourselves, laying down our life for others (Phil 2:3; Jn 15:13). The universe is to be stamped by this dynamic that pervades the Triune God's plan for creation. As the Italian theologian, Piero Coda, puts it,

> Christ makes himself nothing in obedience to the Father and out of love for humankind. The language is certainly metaphoric, but Christian mystics intuited there was something very deep here. The hymn in Paul's letter to the Philippians pushes in the same direction, "Christ though in the form of God, emptied himself, taking the form of a slave, being born in human likeness" (2:7). The love that is revealed in Jesus Christ and called "agape" in the New Testament... is expressed in giving room to the other. And this demands death to oneself, a making oneself nothing, the "kenosis" of which Paul speaks. And this isn't just an intentional or spiritual fact but rather we see here also an ontological meaning. It tells us something about God's being, the being of creation and the relationship between the two.[9]

---

9. Piero Coda, "Creazione" in Piero Coda and Giovanni Filoramo, (eds.), *Dizionario del cristianesimo* (Turin: Utet, 2006), p.267.

In finding its home in God, creation participates in a dynamic of mutual unity and distinction that is exhibited by Jesus Christ on the Cross in his relationship, in the Spirit, to the Father. God does not crush creation's possibilities but, in the power of the Spirit, offers his own inner life of unity in distinction as the realm whereby we can grow and flourish.

In Jn 17, we hear Jesus pray the night before he died, the night he will totally surrender his life in obedience to the Father, that we might share in his glory and in his union with the Father: "so that they may all be one, as you, Father, are in me and I in you, that they also may be in us" (Jn 17:21). In his death and resurrection Jesus Christ draws all of creation with him into the inner dialogue of ever-new vitality and love within the Triune God. As Piero Coda puts it,

> According to Christian revelation, the Son/Word become man lives as creature the same relationship that he has always—on the level of divine being—lived with the Father. With this, he reveals and realizes the intrinsic meaning, dynamic and finality of created being: to become - as the Christian tradition puts it—son in the Son. True, this fact has above all an anthropological meaning—it tells us about the human identity/vocation. But through man, it tells us about the identity/vocation of the whole of creation (as Paul affirms in Rom 8:19–23). The Trinitarian principle of a relationship between God and the world in terms of sonship is thus proposed as a very balanced paradigm in the understanding of the meaning of transcendence and immanence of God with regard to the world... The paradigm suggested by the Trinitarian perspective rethinks the abstract opposition... of transcendence and/or immanence of God and the world, by forwarding an understanding of transcendence that doesn't exclude a specific form of immanence, and of an immanence that presupposes and safeguards transcendence. God's transcendence is so transcendent—if we can put it like this—that it is expressed in the most perfect immanence in creation."[10]

---

10.   Ibid., p. 268.

## Conclusion

In this chapter I have tried to offer some reflection points on the Christian doctrine of creation with particular attention given to the link between creation and the Trinity. I have proposed that in giving humanity freedom to choose how to shape our world, God did not leave us homeless or without a ground plan for our "home." Christian revelation tells us that it is in love that we contribute to the transformation of the universe in accordance with God's plan. As the Second Vatican Council affirmed:

> We do not know the time for the consummation of the earth and of humanity, nor do we know how all things will be transformed... but we are taught that God is preparing a new dwelling place and a new earth where justice will abide, and whose blessedness will answer and surpass all the longings for peace which spring up in the human heart. Then, with death overcome, the sons and daughters of God will be raised up in Christ, and what was sown in weakness and corruption will be invested with incorruptibility. Enduring with charity and its fruits, all that creation which God made on man's account will be unchained from the bondage of vanity.[11]

To fully grasp the fulfillment of creation as distinct from but fully united with the Triune God, we would need "an eternity to explore this Mystery whose riches can never be fathomed."[12] For now, however, it is important to know that we are called to live "on earth as it is in heaven," and that means to "live the Trinity" as Saint John Paul put it some years ago.[13] We do so through the love that seasons our daily tasks and through our love for one another, the love that transforms. To explore this theme further we would need to reflect on the central role of the Eucharist in the transformation of our cosmos. But that is for another day. Suffice to say that the Eucharist, the secret heartbeat of the world, is drawing us into the "new heaven and new earth," prompting us now to order our economics and ecology, our inter-cultural relations and our political order in the light of the Triune God's creative project of love for humanity.

---

11.   *Gaudium et Spes*, 39.
12.   O'Donnell, *Mystery of the Triune God*, p, 167.
13.   See his Apostolic Letter, Novo Millennio Ineunte (6 January, 2001), n. 29.

# 10

# From Beginning to End: The Scientific Relevance of Creation and New Creation

## David Wilkinson

E T.S. WALTON IS THE only Irish winner of the Nobel prize for Physics. He was a colleague of Rutherford at the Cavendish Laboratory in Cambridge and did key work in the splitting of the atom. He was also a committed Christian and Methodist layman. He said:

> One way to learn the mind of the Creator is to study His creation. We must pay God the compliment of studying His work of art and this should apply to all realms of human thought. A refusal to use our intelligence honestly is an act of contempt for Him who gave us that intelligence.[1]

For Walton as with many other scientists from Galileo onwards, science was seen as a gift from God. Indeed their Christian faith energized and inspired their scientific endeavors. They held that God revealed himself both in the book of his Word and the book of his World, and that if the two did not immediately or obviously agree then they would not dismiss one or the other but hold the tension until the science or the interpretation of scripture became clearer.

The culture of today is different. Creation is a hot topic. The onslaught of Richard Dawkins to argue that science is the only sure way to understand questions of the origin of life,[2] contrasts

---

1. Quoted by McBrierty, V. J., *Ernest Thomas Sinton Walton, The Irish Scientist, 1903–1995*, Trinity College Dublin Press, p. 58.
2. Dawkins, R., *The God Delusion*, Bantam Press, London, 2006.

sharply with those who argue that the Universe cannot be understood without taking into account intelligent design.[3] Six day creationism is growing in popularity on both sides of the Atlantic[4] while science pushes the scientific story ever closer to the Big Bang, seemingly removing the need of any first cause.[5] In this controversial area, does the Christian doctrine of creation have anything to say that is relevant or indeed makes sense? In this article we shall outline the doctrine of creation as Christians have understood it and see that it both affirms and critiques all the views of the Universe mentioned above. In this it provides a fruitful way forward in understanding the Universe both scientifically and theologically.

## Speaking with humility

A great deal of the attacks on creation made by Hawking and Dawkins are no more than very old versions of critiques of the cosmological and design arguments. Here the task of Christian theology is to agree with the flaws of the cosmological and design arguments and to show that they are not a part of the basis of belief in the God of the Bible.

Yet there are some areas where new discoveries do raise significant new questions. Hawking in his most recent work provocatively claims that, "philosophy is dead. Philosophy has not kept up with modern developments in science, particularly physics."[6] It reflects a widespread feeling among scientists that there has been a lack of *specific* understanding or engagement with theories such as inflation, string theory or M-theory. Instead, theologians and philosophers continue to assert generalizations about creation. Hawking's comments can also be echoed by those working not on the beginning but the end of the universe. In the twentieth century, which has been characterized by many as a century dominated by theologies of hope,

3.  Dembski, W. A. and Ruse, M. (Eds.), *Debating Design: from Darwin to DNA*, CUP, Cambridge, 2004.
4.  Coleman, S. and Carlin, L. (Eds.), *The Cultures of Creationism: Anti-evolutionism in English Speaking Countries*, Ashgate, Aldershot, 2004.
5.  Hawking, S. W., and L. Mlodinow, *The Grand Design*. London: Bantam, 2010; Krauss, L. M., *A Universe from Nothing: Why There Is Something Rather Than Nothing*, London: Simon & Schuster 2012.
6.  Hawking, S. W., and L. Mlodinow. *The Grand Design*. London: Bantam, 2010, p. 5.

it is remarkable how little direct engagement there has been with the long-term fate of the physical universe. Dan Hardy wrote, "It is partly due to the widespread avoidance of direct engagement with creation and eschatology by theologians... that scientists and those of a speculative turn of mind have turned to such wider issues."[7] Perhaps one of those scientists is the physicist Frank Tipler who wants to "rescue eschatology from the hands of theologians who with a few exceptions...are quite ignorant of it."[8]

To overcome such prejudice and indeed ignorance, dialogue must begin with considerable humility on both sides. It is easy for Christians to point out the laziness of philosophical thinking on the part of Dawkins and Krauss. However, we need to do considerable work also. Cosmology is a rapidly changing subject area with a large degree of dependence on the language of mathematics. This means that it is difficult for theologians to understand and engage. Perhaps a deeper reason is that within Western theology the physical universe is not seen to be important. Greek dualism downplays God's commitment to the physical, salvation is seen as being individual deliverance from the material world, and hope is focused on the existence of the soul in heaven.

In contrast, the Judaeo-Christian view expressed in the Bible sees the physical creation as good, the incarnation and resurrection of Jesus asserts God's commitment not just to human beings but to the physicality of the universe, and Christian hope is for a new heaven and a new earth, a new creation. Being clear about such biblical themes will help us to engage more seriously in the dialogue.[9]

*Recognizing how messy it is*

One of the difficulties in engaging in dialogue is that the scientific picture changes quickly and sometimes dramatically. For example, even up to the middle of the 1990s, cosmologists

---

7.  Hardy, D., 'Creation and Eschatology' in *The Doctrine of Creation*, edited by C. Gunton. Edinburgh: T&T Clark, 1997 p. 112.
8.  Tipler, F. J., *The Physics of Immortality*, London: Weidenfeld & Nicolson, 1994, p. xiii.
9.  See for example Polkinghorne, J. C., *Theology in the Context of Science*. London: SPCK, 2008.

would have described two possibilities for the future of the universe. One would be that the total mass of the universe would reverse the expansion of the Big Bang, gravity taking over in a contraction leading to a Big Crunch. The second would be that the universe would expand forever but would slow down in its expansion rate.

In 1998, astronomers began to look at distant supernova explosions of stars to decide between these two possibilities. In fact their results showed something that was completely unexpected. The universe is accelerating in its rate of expansion due to some unknown type of force, the so-called 'dark energy.'[10] There had been no theoretical prediction of this, apart from Einstein's original inclusion of his cosmological constant in his solution of the equations of general relativity for the universe. It led to near panic among theorists with a range of possible explanations. In fact the interpretation of an accelerating universe propelled by dark energy has been confirmed by more recent results from the Wilkinson Microwave Anisotropy Probe (WMAP).[11] It is a reminder of how provisional the conclusions of cosmology can be and how much weight should be put upon them in theological discourse.

Cosmology is very much a detective story, looking for clues or pieces of evidence which then allow the construction of the best model of what happened in the past and what will happen in the future. It is the weighing of evidence that is crucial in giving a sense of how robust the model is, and this 'art' is quite difficult for the person without research experience in science. Christian theology must stand against the naïve realism of some scientists and the media who present scientific models as the absolute truth on the way the world is. At the same time it is not good enough for Christian apologists to try and gain points in a debate by pointing out that as models change 'they

10. Riess, A., et.al. (1998), 'Observational Evidence from Supernovae for an Accelerating Universe and a Cosmological Constant', *Astron. J.,* 116, 1009; Perlmutter, S., et.al. (1999), 'Measurements of Omega and Lambda from 42 High-Redshift Supernovae', *Astrophys. J.,* 517, 565; Riess, A. G., et.al., (2001), 'The Farthest Known Supernova: Support for an Accelerating Universe and a Glimpse of the Epoch of Deceleration', *Astrophys. J.,* 560, 49–71; Perlmutter, S. (2003), 'Supernovae, Dark Energy, and the Accelerating Universe', *Physics Today,* April 2003, 53–60.
11. Boughn, S. and Crittenden, R. (2004), 'A correlation between the cosmic microwave background and large-scale structure in the universe', *Nature,* 427, 45..

are only a theory'. The reality of cosmology is that it is a messy business, a subtle interplay of theory and observation, human judgement and provisional models which are subject to change as new data is gathered. Models take time to be constructed, tested and questioned by the scientific community, and there will always remain surprises.

In such difficulties, a few theological voices may say that it is not worth the effort for theology to take science seriously. It is here that the importance of recognizing that science is a gift from God—a gift which gives us a critical realist view of the universe. The belief in order in the Universe as described by mathematics began in the Greek culture, but was strengthened by the Christian belief that the Creator was a faithful God. This led to the belief in universal laws of science. These laws enabled scientists to probe back in time and to probe into the future. In all of this, observation, again encouraged strongly by the Christian world-view, took a leading role in determining how good the models were that were suggested.

One of the remarkable things about cosmology is that the surprises that the universe gives us often lead us to seeing that at the heart of everything are the laws of physics, far more beautiful, elegant and simple than we ever expected them to be.

## No need of gaps

Through the messy process of science, one of the great achievements of cosmology has been the Big Bang model of the origin of the universe. It describes the expansion of the universe from a time when it was only $10^{-43}$ seconds old. At that stage, 13.7 billion years ago, the universe was an incredibly dense mass, so small that it could pass through the eye of a needle.

In the book of Job, the Lord says "Where were you when I laid the foundations of the world" and one could ask the same question to cosmologists! Yet this detective story of gathering the evidence and building the best model has worked very well. Three pieces of evidence were crucial. First, early in the twentieth century V.M. Slipher and Edwin Hubble observed that the light from other galaxies displayed a phenomenon called redshift. This occurs when light is emitted by an object which is moving away from us. Hubble then measured the distances to these galaxies and found that the further away they were, the faster they were moving away from us. He interpreted this as the space between the galaxies was expanding. And if it is expanding, it must have expanded from somewhere. Second, in 1965 Arno Penzias and Robert Wilson were attempting another experiment altogether when they detected an 'echo' of the Big Bang, the microwave background radiation. Third, in the 1980s we were able to measure the amount of helium in the universe which is a good test of theoretical models of the Big Bang and it was in good agreement with predictions.

Yet not all of the questions concerning the Big Bang can be answered. Observations by the Wilkinson Microwave Anisotropy satellite have confirmed our overall picture of the Big Bang, but have also reminded us how much we still need to find out. As we have already discussed a large proportion of the universe is in the form of dark energy (over 70%) and at the moment we have little idea as to what it is. Another 23% of the universe is also in the form of dark matter—we know it is there but we are not sure what it is. The fact that we know only a tiny fraction therefore of what the universe is made of is somewhat embarrassing for cosmologists! Yet the power of science is that we know what we do not know, and we are able to design experiments at the Large Hadron Collider which might at least tell us what the dark matter is.

Nevertheless there are questions which are much more difficult. The standard model of the hot Big Bang describes the origin of the Universe as an expansion from a singularity, that is, a point of infinite density. But that singularity raises immediate problems. First, general relativity which describes the expansion of the universe so well suggests that time is not completely independent of space, and that gravity is then explained as a consequence of this space-time being curved by the distribution of mass-energy in it. Thus the distribution of mass determines the geometry of space and the rate of flow of time. However, at a singularity there is infinite density and infinite curvature of space-time. General relativity is unable to cope with this infinity and predicts its own downfall, that is, the theory breaks down at the singularity. Second, general relativity as a theory is inconsistent with quantum theory. General relativity, which is extremely successful in describing the large scale structure of the Universe needs to specify mass and its position in order to then describe the geometry and rate of flow of time. At a singularity where the gravitational field is so strong, and the whole Universe is so small that it is on the atomic scale of quantum theory, it is believed that quantum effects should be important. Quantum theory, however, says that you can never know both the mass and position without an intrinsic uncertainty. You cannot have both general relativity and quantum theory to describe a situation.

The singularity problem therefore is that general relativity is unable to give a description of the singularity, or in other words, the initial conditions of the expansion of the Universe. To put it another way, present scientific theories are unable to predict what will come out of the singularity. They can describe the subsequent expansion but are unable to reach back beyond an age of $10^{-43}$ seconds to zero. This 'limit' of scientific theory, unable to reach back to the very beginning, was frustrating to physicists but attractive to some theologians. Is God needed to 'fix' the initial conditions of the Universe? If science is unable to describe the initial moments, is this 'the gap' where God comes in to set the Universe off?

However, many scientists resist this trajectory. Hawking attempts to use the laws of physics to explain not just the evolution of the universe but also its initial conditions. In order to do this you have to bring quantum theory and general relativity together into a quantum theory of gravity. Such a theory he suggests can explain how the blue touch paper of the Big Bang lights itself. The core of Hawking's theory, in John Barrow's phrase, is that, "once upon a time there was no time."[12] Hawking is saying that the Universe does have a beginning but it does not need a cause for in the theory the notion of time melts away. Hawking's universe emerges from a fluctuation in a quantum field. No cause as such is necessary.

Hawking believes that the best candidate to do this is M-theory, which is in fact a whole family of different theories where each theory applies to phenomena within a certain range. It suggests 11 dimensions of space time. However for Hawking it also

12. J.D. Barrow, *The Observer*, 7th May 1993.

suggests that our universe is one in $10^{500}$ universes which arise naturally from physical law, that is, "their creation does not require the intervention of some supernatural being or god."[13]

It must be stressed that Hawking's thinking on this is not fully accepted by the rest of the scientific community. There are other proposals on how to deal with the problem of the laws breaking down, and it remains difficult to know whether quantum theory can be applied to the whole Universe.

If Hawking's attempt to explain scientifically the first moment of the Universe's history is indeed successful, then this rightly demolishes a god of the gaps. The God of Christian theology is not a God who fills in any gaps of current scientific ignorance, nor interacts with the very first moment of the Universe's history and then retires a safe distance. Hawking's use of M-theory may eventually work, but the Christian theologian while applauding enthusiastically, will also raise the question of where does M-theory itself come from. God is the one who creates and sustains the laws of physics, which science assumes but does not explain.

Such a god of the gaps argument has sometimes been used in apologetic arguments to try and prove the existence of God. The argument that the Big Bang needs God to start it off, is an argument called the cosmological argument in temporal form and has been used in different contexts for centuries. It has however a number of weaknesses. Augustine had pointed out many years ago that the Universe was created with time not in time. Therefore to ask the question what came *before* the Universe is attempting to use the concept of time before it came into existence! In addition, the first cause argument derives from a notion that the Universe is a thing or event. Now it is easy to say everything has cause, but is the Universe a thing or event?

More importantly, as scientists explain more and more about the Universe, so there is a temptation to look for unexplained gaps in the knowledge of the natural world in order to find space for God. But this 'god of the gaps' is always in danger of becoming irrelevant as science fills in more of its own story. In contrast, the Bible understands that the whole Universe is the

---

13. Hawking, S. W., and L. Mlodinow, *The Grand Design*, London: Bantam, 2010, p. 8.

result of God's working. God is at much at work at the first $10^{-43}$ second as at any other time. A scientific description of that moment in time does not invalidate it as being the activity of God as any other event.

This in fact leads us on to another key point.

*Theism not deism*

Too often Christians have viewed the Creator God in deistic terms not theistic terms. The deists believed in a God who set off the universe and then went for a cup of coffee not having anything more to do with it. Perhaps this has been motivated by first cause arguments for the existence of God, and perhaps it has been due to viewing the Christian theology of creation as built simply on the first chapters of the book of Genesis.

However, the biblical material is much broader and richer. Genesis needs to be seen alongside passages such as Proverbs 8:22–36 and Job 38:1–42:17 which stress the wisdom of God in creation, passages which celebrate the glory and majesty of God (Psalm 8, 19, 148, Isaiah 40:9–31), and passages which look forward to new creation (Isaiah 65:17–25, Romans 8:18–27, 2 Peter 3:3–13, Revelation 21:1–8).[14] In this latter regard, of course, central to the New Testament is the role of Christ in creation (John 1:1–18, Colossians 1:15–20, Hebrews 1:1–14), regarded as the word or wisdom of God through whom all was spoken and in whom all are destined to find their authentic voice. In all of these passages, it is clear that creation is not the subject of pure intellectual speculation, but is used to convey a message about God and God's relationship with the world. Here cosmology is rarely of interest for its own sake.

While the interest of the modern world may be on how the theology of creation relates to scientific cosmology, the biblical writers were concerned with something very different—with the meaning of things in God's providential plan

Take, for example, the depiction of Christ at the heart of creation in Colossians 1:15–20. Here we find applied to Jesus everything that could be said of the figure of 'wisdom' in creation (Proverbs 8:22). The implication is that at the heart of creation

---

14. Wilkinson, D., *Creation*. The Bible Speaks Today Bible Themes, Leicester: IVP, 2002.

is not simply a divine attribute but a divine personality. Christ is proclaimed here as "the firstborn over all creation" (v.15), signifying supreme rank or that he is prior in importance. Nor is Christ simply a part of the created order, "for by him all things were created" (v.16). Creation, in this view, is the activity of God the Father in the Son: not only do all things have their origin in Christ, "in him all things hold together" (v.17). The verb is in the perfect tense indicating that 'everything' has held together in him and continues to do so, that through him the world is sustained and prevented from falling into chaos. The source of the universe's unity, order and consistency is to be found, Colossians is suggesting, in the continuing work of God in Christ.

Far, then, from cosmology being in conflict with Christian faith, it is properly affirmed by Christian theology given that the whole of the created order is thought of as owing its origin, purpose and continued existence to Christ. Indeed, in this way of thinking, the exploration or use of the order in the Universe is only possible because of Christ.

This is a further insight into God's relationship with the universe. The biblical images are not of a deistic god who breaks a bottle against the hull of the universe and then waves it off into the distance saying, "Good-bye—see you on judgement day." "In him all things together" gives much more a picture of God as the one who keeps the universe afloat and together. God is the basis of the natural order, the basis of the physical laws. In John Polkinghorne's phrase he is the guarantee of the physical equations by which the universe develops. This is much more the God of Christian theism rather than deism. Don Page, a long-time collaborator of Hawking, sums this up:

> God creates and sustains the entire Universe rather than just the beginning. Whether or not the Universe has a beginning has no relevance to the question of its creation, just as whether an artist's line has a beginning and an end, or instead forms a circle with no end, has no relevance to the question of its being drawn.[15]

---

15. Page, D., 'Hawking's timely story', *Nature*, 1998, 333, pp. 742–3.

## Word and works

In this critique of god of the gaps and deism, Hawking and others may be pushing Christians back to their biblical roots. God is not proved through philosophical arguments. God is known through his self-revelation in becoming a human being in Jesus Christ. Karl Barth put it bluntly:

> I believe in Jesus Christ, God's Son our Lord, in order to perceive and to understand that God the Almighty, the Father, is Creator of heaven and earth. If I did not believe the former, I could not perceive and understand the latter.[16]

This conviction underpinned Barth's hostility to any idea of natural theology which starts outside of revelation and is not a result of grace. For many other theologians Barth pushes his argument too far at this point in denying that humans have the ability to see something of the Creator in creation itself and in appearing not to value the physical creation as anything other than as a backdrop to God's activities.

From the beginning of the scientific revolution, Christian thinkers such as Francis Bacon saw God revealing himself in both the book of his Word and in the book of his works. This knowledge of God through the universe was never enough for salvation but it did expand our perspective of the nature of God.

It is interesting that in the last four decades of cosmology, a number of scientists have been led to a range of philosophical and theological questions. While science has been extremely successful, the Universe it has revealed seems to pose questions which go beyond science. This is particularly fascinating when these questions are asked by cosmologists such as Paul Davies who would not share any Christian commitment.

What have these scientists responded to? First, there is the question of *the purpose of the Universe*. Leibniz had of course asked many years ago why is there something rather than nothing? This is not to resurrect the first cause argument, it is to recognize that the purpose and meaning of the Universe lie beyond science. The Christian will argue they find a natural answer in a personal God. Second, the question of *the origin of the scientific*

---

16. Barth, K., *Church Dogmatics Vol III*, edited by G. W. Bromiley and T. F. Torrance. Edinburgh: T&T Clark, 1958, p. 29.

*laws.* If the Universe emerges as a quantum fluctuation, we need to ask where quantum theory itself comes from? Where does the pattern of the world come from and how is it maintained? This is not a 'god of the gaps' argument as science itself assumes these laws in order to work. Once again the Christian will argue the Creator God is the natural answer. Third, the *question of the intelligibility of the Universe.* Why does the mathematics of our minds resonate with the mathematics of the Universe expressed in the laws of physics. A number of physicists find the beauty, simplicity, universality and intelligibility of the laws of physics themselves to be pointers to this universe having a 'deeper story' to its existence. Fourth, the question of *anthropic balances.* Paul Davies characterizes this as *The Goldilocks Enigma,*[17] that is, balances in the circumstances and laws of the universe that make it just right for the emergence of intelligent life. This can be illustrated in the extraordinary fine tuning of numbers fundamental to the universe, such as the ratio of the electric force to the gravitational force; how firmly atomic nuclei bind together; the ratio of energy needed to disperse an object compared to its total rest mass energy; and the number of spatial dimensions in the universe. If any of these numbers were only slightly different to what they are we would not be here. While this cannot become a proof of the existence of a Creator, some of these balances are so extraordinary that for many people they point to some kind of purpose in the universe. Fifth, the question of *awe.* Whether in response to the dramatic photographs of the universe taken by the Hubble Space Telescope or in those moments when the scientist sees that underneath the complexity of the universe are a few elegant laws, this sense of awe for many resonates with, "The heavens declare the glory of God" (Psalm 19:1).

None of these insights into the way the world is can be promoted to proofs of the existence of a Creator God. For example, anthropic balances have an alternative explanation to the design of God. This explanation is that the anthropic principle selects this universe out of many. We see this fine-tuning because we are here. In other universes where these numbers were different there would be no one there to see them. While there are many theories of many universes, there is considerable debate as to

17. Davies, Paul, *The Goldilocks Enigma: Why Is the Universe Just Right for Life?* London: Allen Lane, 2006.

whether other universe speculation is metaphysics or physics. Can we know that they are there by the passing of information from one universe to another, or do we accept their existence on the basis of the prediction of theories which solve other problems to do with our early universe? Such speculation about the existence of other universes cautions us against resurrecting the proof of design argument. As long as we lack of physical evidence for other universes, it remains metaphysical speculation, and an alternative explanation to that of a Creator God.

Anthropic balances and other insights do not prove the existence of a Creator, but they do provoke questions and for some are pointers to the existence of a Creator. These questions and pointers find answers and are integrated into a consistent picture from the perspective of a Creator who is revealed in the life, death and resurrection of Jesus Christ.

## Beginnings and new beginnings

Earlier in the paper we noted the contemporary importance of work on the long term future of the universe and some of the theological questions it raises. These have often been neglected due to a focus on origins in the dialogue of theology and cosmology. Yet the work of Perlmutter, Riess and Schmidt recognized in the award of the Nobel prize, asks the Christian the question of how can God's purposes be seen in the light of an accelerating universe leading to heat death.

Today, cosmology looks ahead with pessimism rather than optimism. It points to a future of futility for the physical and with it the end of the survival of intelligent life within the universe. An accelerated heat death is a bleak end. When the universe is $10^{12}$ years old, stars cease to form, as there is no hydrogen left. At this stage all massive stars have now turned into neutron stars and black holes. At $10^{14}$ years, small stars become white dwarfs. The universe becomes a cold and uninteresting place composed of dead stars and black holes.

As might be expected science has attempted to provide some optimism and indeed salvation for human life. Dyson and Tipler are struck by the ability of humans in manipulating the environment of the Earth and wonder if this could be extrapolated forward. Dyson suggested that biological life would adapt first through genetic engineering to redesign organisms that could cope in such a universe. Then consciousness would be transferred to new kinds of hardware that would be able to cope with the ultra-low temperatures of a heat death universe, including for example a complex dust cloud. In this way "life and intelligence are potentially immortal."[18] Tipler sees consciousness transferred to computers which expand across space. He argues that it is possible on such a model that a point will be reached when an infinite or maximum amount of information will have been processed, and 'life' has expanded everywhere in the universe.[19] However, both Dyson and Tipler's models cannot cope with an accelerating Universe. Science cannot change the prediction that the future of the universe itself is futility.

Paul Davies suggests that an "almost empty universe growing steadily more cold and dark for all eternity is profoundly depressing."[20]

Some theologians will say that this is so far in the future that it is irrelevant, while others have concentrated their thinking on the future of the Earth, the individual believer or the church. However, what biblical themes might be important for thinking about the future of the physical universe that might give hope?

First we note the importance of the theme of new creation within a range of biblical genres. In Revelation the vision is of "a new heaven and a new earth" (Rev 21:1). This is not about some other worldly existence which has no connection with the physical universe. It is about God doing something with the totality of existence. At the same time it is about something new, not about keeping this creation alive for as long as possible which is the hope of the 'eschatological scientists' such as Dyson and Tipler.

Second, new creation is a possibility because of a Creator God. The new creation is continually linked to God's original creative work, and hope for the future is built on an understanding of God as Creator (Is 65:17–25). Whatever the circumstances, creation is not limited to its own inherent possibilities

18. Dyson, F., *Infinite in All Directions,* New York : Harper & Row, 1988.
19. Tipler, F. J., *The Physics of Immortality,* London: Weidenfeld & Nicolson, 1994.
20. Davies, P., 'Eternity: Who Needs It?' in *The Far Future Universe: Eschatology from a Cosmic Perspective,* ed. Ellis, G. F. R., Radnor: Templeton Foundation Press, 2002, p. 48.

because the God of creation is still at work. A God who is not free to work in the Universe must watch the slow heat death of creation. Bauckham rightly attacks models of providence that make God dependent on the Universe:

> A God who is not the transcendent origin of all things but a way of speaking of the immanent creative possibilities of the universe itself cannot be the ground of ultimate hope for the future of creation. Where faith in God the Creator wanes, so inevitably does hope for the resurrection, let alone the new creation of all things.[21]

The scientific predictions of the end of the universe are a reminder that models of providence have to take seriously the universe over its entire history, rather than just the present state of the Universe. Models that stress immanence too much at the expense of transcendence face a bleak future in the end of the universe. At the extreme limit of this, models where God is a superior intelligence totally contained in the universe, as have been developed by some scientists in a revamped natural theology, become gods who eventually will die.[22] Likewise, models that stress God's non-intervention in the universe are presented with an interesting question in terms of the end of the universe. For example, Wiles' model sees God simply sustaining the creative process of the universe, limiting himself not to act in the world in any particular way.[23] The question then arises of why is God sustaining a process that will end in futility?

Third, creation and new creation are mutually interdependent and find their focus of connection in Jesus Christ (Col 1:15–20). This is a reminder of something that should be obvious but in practice is often forgotten. Creation needs to be seen in the light of new creation, and new creation needs to be seen in the light of creation. A great deal of work in the dialogue of science and religion has concentrated on the doctrine of creation with little reference to the end of the story. The suffering, frustration and decay of this world show that this creation

21. Bauckham, R., *The Theology of the Book of Revelation*, Cambridge: CUP, 1993, p. 51.
22. Dick, S. J., 'Cosmotheology: Theological Implications of the New Universe', in *Many Worlds: The New Universe, Extraterrestrial Life and the Theological Implications* ed. Dick, S. J. Radnor: Templeton Foundation Press, 2000, pp. 191–208.
23. Wiles, M., *God's Action in the World*, London: SCM, 1986.

is both necessary and points forward to a new creation (Rom 8:18–30).

Fourth, new creation is a transformation of the present creation rather than a total annihilation and beginning again. Bauckham is correct in seeing such passages as 2 Pt 3:10–13 in the context of Jewish apocalyptic. In contrast to dissolving and renewing fire of the Stoics, and the Zoroastrian view of purification, here the emphasis is on judgement. Bauckham concludes that such passages "emphasize the radical discontinuity between the old and the new, but it is nevertheless clear that they intend to describe a renewal not an abolition of creation."[24]

Fifth, God is at work towards new creation both in the process and in the particular event. The second coming of Christ reminds us that biblical eschatology has a focus on Jesus Christ, and further the images used are suggestive of an eschatological event, which is both in space and time, and yet transcends space and time (1 Th 4:13–5:11). It is a reminder of the importance of the particular action of God within God's more general activity of sustaining and transforming. Thus the redemption of this creation is pictured in terms of a long process, working through contemporary structures, as well as a specific event of judgement.

Sixth, the resurrection of Jesus is the model by which the continuity and discontinuity between creation and new creation is held together. If as Paul argues, the resurrection is the first-fruits of God's transformative work, then there should be both continuity and discontinuity in the relationship of creation and new creation as there was in the relationship of Jesus before the cross and Jesus risen. The empty tomb is a sign that God's purposes for the material world are that it should be transformed not discarded. If resurrection affirms creation, then it also points forward to new creation.

Continuity and discontinuity in the transformation of the physical Universe may be located in the nature of matter, space and time. To take time as an example, the resurrected Jesus does not seem limited by space and time. In new creation the continuity may be that time is real but the discontinuity is that time no longer limits us in the way that it does in this creation.

---

24. Bauckham, R., *Jude 2 Peter,* Waco: Texas, 1983, p. 326.

It could be argued that the resurrection body is characterized by decay's reversal, that is, a purposeful flourishing. In this creation time is associated with decay and growth, but in new creation might time be simply about growth? We are therefore suggesting that our experience of time in the physical Universe is a small and limited part of an ontologically real time that we might call eternity.

Seventh, the Spirit's work both in the church and the world is transformative. Pannenberg's conviction is that the work of the Spirit needs to be seen as dynamic and as giving priority to the whole over parts. He wants to see the Spirit as giving cohesiveness to the Universe. Indeed, the work of the Spirit could be seen as giving cohesiveness to the work of new creation. Perhaps the Spirit is the ground and the redeemer of the relationality inherent in the Universe. Can we therefore see signs of the Spirit restoring damage and progressing God's work on to completion? This may be an area which has had a lot of attention in terms of the Spirit's work in the life of the believer, but how do we see it in the cosmic context? In Paul's discussion in Romans 8, that the Spirit works in the tension between creation and new creation, sharing in the 'groaning' of this creation and yet pointing forward to the hope of that which is to come. Yet the Spirit's work is more than that. If the damage of sin is the breaking of relationships between Creator, creatures and creation, then is the Spirit's work of restoring those relationships in part a sign of the final reconciliation of a new heaven and a new earth? Restored relationships now in terms of individual forgiveness, community reconciliation, the care of animals and responsibility for the environment then become signs of God's purposes for the whole of creation.

These seven points set out a structure for dialogue. They do not set out to map the biblical account exactly onto the scientific account, or to see them as completely independent. The Christian will come to the scientific description of the future of the physical universe with much to learn but also much to offer.

The distinguished cosmologist Martin Rees comments, "What happens in far-future aeons may seem blazingly irrelevant to the practicalities of our lives. But I don't think the cosmic context is entirely irrelevant to the way we perceive our

Earth and the fate of humans."[25] This is a challenge to all theologians, not least those who take openness seriously.

A Christian theology of creation maintains that this creation really is good, whilst also looking forward in the purposes of God to a new creation. This hope of a new creation is not of God completely starting again, or the hope for some kind of disembodied immaterial state, but the hope for the transfiguring fulfillment of this present creation into all that it was called into being to be. Given this combination of identity and transformation, the present created order is not to be written off as evil or unimportant, but is, rather, to be cared for, respected, enjoyed and delighted in.

25. Rees, M., *Our Final Hour,* New York : Basic Books, , 2003, p. 4.